GROWING
Like Jesus

Student Activity Book

GROWING
Like Jesus

Student Activity Book

---

52 Reproducible In-Class Activities and Family Devotionals

wph wesleyan
publishing
house

Indianapolis, Indiana

Copyright © 2006 by Wesleyan Publishing House
Published by Wesleyan Publishing House
Indianapolis, Indiana 46250
Printed in the United States of America

ISBN-13: 978-0-89827-341-0
ISBN-10: 0-89827-341-2

Written by Rodney Wasson and Colleen Derr.

How to Use This Book

Our children's spiritual formation is critical and encompasses the development of their heart, head, and habits. The Building Faith Kids Series is designed to be a supplemental tool to assist you in this development by providing Biblical knowledge, Scripture memory verses, and general truths about God. Understand that spiritual formation is a life-long endeavor; it requires intentional instruction, modeled behavior, reinforcement from home, and open hearts and minds.

This Student Activity Book is intended to come alongside the Building Faith Kids leader manual and allow students to deepen their grasp of the content, connect the belief to their everyday life, and receive reinforcement from home through family-friendly applications. Every lesson corresponds directly to the lesson in the Building Faith Kids leader manual and is reproducible and ready for distribution among your students.

The In-Class Activity Page contains:

Concept and Teaching Points

What Do You Think?—a time to reflect on the belief and then demonstrate understanding through a response.

Challenge—an opportunity to act on the belief through a life response.

Did You Know?—a trivia statement that is connected to the lesson.

The Family Devotions Page contains:

Talk About It—a question-prompt to create conversation and dialogue.

Think About It—a family devotional centered around a Scripture text that supports the concept.

Pray About It—a unique family-prayer-time idea.

Live It—an interactive family-challenge that reinforces the concept with a physical response.

Memorize It—a creative idea on how to learn the memory verse as a family.

Learning Concepts

God

1. There is only one God.
2. God is greater than anything.
3. God made the world from nothing.
4. God cares about all people.
5. God is perfect, fair, and faithful.
6. God is everywhere all the time.
7. God is all-knowing.
8. God is all-powerful.
9. We talk with God through prayer.
10. God wants us to worship and praise Him.

Scripture

11. The Bible is God's Word.
12. The Bible shows us who God is and what He has done.
13. God's Word never changes.
14. The Bible tells us how to live.

Self

15. I am created in the image of God.
16. I am unique and valuable to God.
17. I am responsible for my choices.
18. God wants my thoughts and actions to be pure.
19. I can use my talents and abilities to please God.

Jesus

20. Jesus is the Son of God.
21. Jesus lived on earth.
22. Jesus is both God and human.
23. Jesus was tempted but did not sin.
24. Jesus came to be our savior.
25. Jesus died on the cross.
26. God raised Jesus from the dead.

Salvation

27. All people have done wrong.
28. Sin separates people from God.
29. God loves us even though we have sinned.
30. God sent his son to forgive our sins.
31. Jesus died to forgive my sin.
32. God forgives those who believe in Jesus.
33. We are adopted into God's family by faith.
34. We can live forever in heaven.

The Church

35. The Church is all believers everywhere.
36. We belong to a local church.
37. Baptism represents our new life in Christ.
38. The Lord's Supper represents Christ's sacrifice.
39. We serve others by helping at church.
40. We support the church with our tithes.
41. The Church spreads the gospel around the world.
42. Christians pray for one another.
43. Christians meet together for worship.

The Christian Life

44. God sent the Holy Spirit to help us.
45. The Holy Spirit helps us understand the truth.
46. The Holy Spirit helps us obey God.
47. The Holy Spirit helps us serve others.
48. We grow stronger by learning God's Word.
49. We grow stronger by praying to God.
50. Christians help those in need.
51. Living for Jesus makes life better.
52. Jesus will come back and take us to heaven.

God

1 There is only one God.

- There is only one God.
- There are no other gods.
- God wants us to put Him first in our life.

DID YOU KNOW?

The Bible was written by forty different authors all pointing to the same true God.

What do YOU think?

What are things that people sometimes make more important than God?

What are some things that you might make more important than God?

Why is it so easy to love things more than we love God?

Challenge

Think about one thing you own that you love more than you should. What will you do about it?

God

1 There is only one God.

TALK about it

What happens when we love stuff more than we love God?

Think About It

Read Deuteronomy 6:1–9. As the people of Israel prepared to go to the land God had promised them, Moses gathered all the people. He reminded them of the Ten Commandments, and he told them to not forget that "the Lord is one." The people were to do everything they could to remember because they would soon have a life filled with new temptations. They would meet people who believed differently than they did, and God knew they could easily be influenced by others. We have the same temptations today. Many people do not believe the same things we believe, and we can easily be influenced to make material things more important than God. Like the children of Israel we need to remind ourselves that things will go well for us when we put God first. What do you spend time or money on? Is it more important than God?

Memorize It

Print each word of the verse on an index card. Make a set for each family member. Shuffle and scatter the cards around the room. Race to complete the verse in the right order.

Hear O Israel:
The LORD our God,
the LORD is one.
Deuteronomy 6:4

Pray About It

Write a family prayer, asking God to help keep Him in first place. Tape the prayer to your doorframe. Read it every time you enter or leave your house.

Building Kids FAITH Series

God

2 God is greater than anything.

- **God is greater than anything.**
- **God created everything.**
- **God is greater than the things He created.**
- **We worship God because He alone is worthy.**

DID YOU KNOW?

The smartest computers in the world don't come close to the power and complexity of your brain.

What do YOU think?

What do you think is the greatest thing God created? Why?

When you think about created things, what do they tell you about God?

Think about something very small. Now think of something very large. Do you think it took God longer to make one or the other? Why or why not?

Challenge

What problem in your life seems too big for you? Remember that God is bigger than anything; ask for His help every day this week.

God

2 God is greater than anything.

TALK about it

Let everyone tell what they think is the greatest thing about God.

Think About It

Read Genesis 1. God said over and over in this chapter, "It is good." At no point did God have to start over; nothing needed to be fixed. All things God made were good, but when He finished creating Adam and Eve He said it was very good. We worship a powerful God who can create by simply thinking or speaking things into being. There is no power like Him. There is no god like our God, but even with all that power, He still takes time to care for you and me. Check out Psalm 135. Our God deserves our praise because there is nothing on earth, in space, or anywhere in the universe like God. He loves us!

Memorize It

Tape this verse to the inside and outside of each bedroom door. Make it the first and last thing you read every day. Try to say the verse, without looking at it, by Wednesday.

This is what the LORD says— Israel's King and Redeemer, the LORD Almighty: I am the first and I am the last; apart from me there is no God.
Isaiah 44:6

Pray About It

Have every family member say a one-sentence prayer, thanking God for one thing. Keep a list of everything you mention. Praise God as you watch the list grow.

God

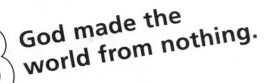

3 ## God made the world from nothing.

- God existed before creation.
- God made the world from nothing.
- God made the world by speaking it into existence.

What do YOU think?

When you come up with creative ideas, how do you communicate them best?

Is it with words, song, pictures, art, or some other way?

Use your favorite form of creativity to express your thoughts about God's creativity.

DID YOU KNOW?

There are close to six and a half billion people on the planet. Each one is God's unique creation.

Challenge

Every time you are outside this week, look at God's creations and try to discover something new. Remember to give thanks and praise.

God

3 God made the world from nothing.

TALK
about it

Can we make anything by just thinking it? In what ways can we create things?

Think About It

Read Psalm 145:1–11. What a wonderful psalm about a wonderful God. When we stop and think about places that make us say, "wow," it is usually a large object in nature, like a mountain or a waterfall. Sometimes we are amazed by something small and complex, like a snowflake or a brain cell. Man-made "stuff" never compares to the things God made. Stop and think about some cool things people have made. Guess what? Everything we make comes from something God made. We can't make anything out of nothing. God made everything out of nothing! Only God deserves our praise and worship.

Memorize It

Have each family member repeat the verse at the beginning of each meal this week and mention one part of creation you think is really cool.

In the beginning God created the heavens and the earth.
Genesis 1:1

Pray About It

Make a list of the different colors and shades you see outside. How many different greens do you see? How many different reds? Thank God for His incredible creativity.

Building Kids FAITH Series

God

4 God cares about all people.

- God loves all His creation.
- God thinks and feels and has a name.
- God created us to love Him and others.
- God wants to take care of His creation.

What do YOU think?

Do you know of a music star or famous athlete who takes time to talk to fans and sign autographs? How do you think the fans feel? How many celebrities, rock stars, or professional athletes do you know that take the time to get to know personally all of their fans? God does! Write a fan letter to God in the space below.

DID YOU KNOW?

Jewish writers used to only write some of the letters in God's name because they thought His name was too holy to write the whole name.

Challenge

Explore your Bible and find as many different names for God as you can. Hint—start with the concordance at the back of your Bible.

Building Kids FAITH Series

God

4 God cares about all people.

TALK about it

Who is the most important person you know? Do they love you? Who does love you?

Think About It

Read Psalm 8. When we consider that God made and put everything in place, we can understand His power and His greatness. When we think about the fact that He made every person and that He loves us, we should feel humble, thankful, and full of worship. Do you ever feel lonely or unloved? Remember God loves you. Do you ever feel stupid or useless? Remember God doesn't make mistakes. Do you ever feel afraid? Remember God cares for you. You are valuable to Him. Still not convinced? Read Matthew 6:25–34.

Memorize It

Whoever turns on the television says the verse and chooses another person to repeat it back to them. Do this every time you watch television this week.

For God so loved the world that he gave his one and only Son, that whoever believes in him shall not perish but have eternal life.
John 3:16

Pray About It

Have everyone point out things that are special about each family member. Thank God for those special things.

Building Kids FAITH Series

God

5 **God is perfect, fair, and faithful.**

- God's goodness is reflected in His holiness and love working together.
- God is perfect.
- God is fair.
- God is faithful.

What do YOU think?

Imagine you just scored the winning touchdown, but you stepped out of bounds. Would you want the referee to be fair? Would you tell him you stepped out of bounds if he didn't see it? Why or why not?

DID YOU KNOW?

God used 12 different judges to help Israel.

Challenge

This week keep track of how many times you hear, "That's not fair!" Remember to thank God for being a fair, faithful God.

Building Kids FAITH Series

God

5 God is perfect, fair, and faithful.

TALK about it

Share a story about someone who wasn't treated fairly and how it made you feel.

Think About It

Have someone read Deuteronomy 32:3–4. Have you ever been to a game where the officials made mistakes or it didn't seem like they were fair? Have you seen trials where everyone thought the judge made a mistake? Have you ever heard your sister or brother whine, "That's not fair"? Has it ever been you whining? We all want the world to be fair; but let's face it, sometimes it isn't. That's why it is so very good to know that our God is always fair. He never makes mistakes. A referee like that we can trust. A judge like that we can trust. A God like that we can trust. "As for God, his way is perfect; the word of the LORD is flawless. He is a shield for all who take refuge in him" (Psalm 18:30).

Memorize It

Stand in a circle. Have someone say the first word; go around, with each person saying the next word in the verse. Start over at the beginning of the verse when a mistake is made.

The LORD is gracious and compassionate; slow to anger and rich in love. The LORD is good to all; he has compassion on all he has made. Psalm 145:8–9

Pray About It

As you pray today, remind everyone that God is perfect, fair and faithful. He is waiting to hear your prayer. He always answers with what is best for us.

Building Kids Faith Series

God

6 God is everywhere all the time.

- God reveals himself in creation and history.
- God reveals himself in Scripture and in Jesus Christ.
- God is present and near to us all the time.

What do YOU think?

What are some times and places you feel God near to you? What are times or places you feel far away from God? Why do you feel close or far from God? Which do you prefer?

DID YOU KNOW?

The approximate amount of Bibles that were published by 1932 was 1,330,213,815.

Challenge

Make two lists. On one, list things you can do to stay close to God. On the other, list things you should avoid.

God

6 God is everywhere
all the time.

TALK
about it

Name different
things that you know
are real, including
things you have
never seen.

Think About It

Pick up a Bible, open it to almost any page,
and you will see God revealing himself to you.
Sometimes you have to look harder than others, but He is
on every page. In the life, death, and resurrection of Jesus, God
revealed himself to us. Read 1 John 4:9. Here is something to think
about. Do you have to think about breathing in order to be able to take a
breath? What about blinking? Even the way God designed us reveals how He
cares for us. He has thought out every single detail. We did not get this way by
accident or evolution; we got this way by design. Check out Acts 17:28.

Memorize It

Pair up and stand facing each other across a large
room. Repeat the verse out loud, taking a step
towards each other with each word. Choose new
partners and repeat daily.

Come near to God and
he will come near to you.
James 4:8

Pray About It

Find a copy of the song "Every Move I
Make" (David Ruis). Read the words or
sing the song as an act of worship and
thanksgiving.

Building **Kids**
FAITH
Series

God

1 God is all-knowing.

- God has unsurpassing knowledge.
- God is wise in His understanding and knowledge.
- God knows me.
- God is all-knowing.

DID YOU KNOW?

Proverbs is a book of wise advice for daily living. There is a chapter for each day of the month.

What do YOU think?

Who are three people you would want on your team in an intelligence contest?

Would you take the same people if it was a test of strength? Why not?

How can you tell when someone is wise?

Challenge

We tend to ask God for help when we haven't studied enough. This week ask Him for wisdom every day on your way to school.

Building Faith Kids Series

God

1 God is all-knowing.

TALK about it

If you could think of the perfect hiding place, where would it be?

Think About It

This is one of those bad news-good news stories. God knows everything. We can't hide from Him. Read Psalm 139. The writer had some of the same thoughts. There is no place to hide from God. That's the bad news if you're doing something wrong and need to hide from God! Do you want the good news? We don't have to hide from God. He loves us even though He knows everything about us, and when things get hard we can hide in Him. Read that psalm again—it's really cool. God is all-knowing and all-wise; when we need wisdom, all we have to do is ask. Check out James 1:5, "If any of you lacks wisdom, he should ask God, who gives generously to all without finding fault, and it will be given to him."

Memorize It

Write the verse around the edge of a piece of paper. Each day draw a picture representing one of the following words: depth, riches, wisdom, knowledge, judgment, paths. Explain how the words relate to God.

Oh, the depth of the riches of the wisdom and knowledge of God! How unsearchable his judgments, and his paths beyond tracing out!
Romans 11:33

Pray About It

Play a quick game of hide 'n seek. As you find each person, thank God for being your hiding place. Thank Him that we don't have to hide from Him.

God

8 God is all-powerful.

- God is all-powerful.
- God's power is shown by His goodness and love.
- God helps us to be what He wants us to be.

What do YOU think?

If you could be a superhero, who would you be? Why?

How do you think God wants you to use the power He has available for you?

DID YOU KNOW?

The word "God" appears 3,358 times in the Bible, but the book of Esther doesn't mention "God" even once.

Challenge

This week write a paragraph or two describing how your life would be different if you let God lead every part of your life.

Building Kids FAITH Series

God

8 God is all-powerful.

TALK about it
What test would you give to find the world's most powerful person?

Think About It

Read Ephesians 1:15–23. Take turns reading so everyone reads a few verses. Did you ever notice that some people use power to control people? This causes some people to fear power. God has the power to completely control us, but He doesn't. He uses power to protect us. He uses it to help us grow if we let Him. The power that raised Christ from the dead is available to us. When we need protection, His power is available. When we feel like the enemy is attacking us, God's power is there for us. When we are weak, we can get stronger with His power. Check out 2 Corinthians 12:9, "But he said to me, 'My grace is sufficient for you, for my power is made perfect in weakness.'" In your weakness, go to Him.

Memorize It

Go for a family walk. Point out cool things God has made. Repeat the verse together every time you point something out.

For since the creation of the world God's invisible qualities—his eternal power and divine nature—have been clearly seen, being understood from what has been made, so that men are without excuse.
Romans 1:20

Pray About It

Where do you need to feel God's power? Pray for it every day this week, then watch Him work in your life. Keep track of His answers to your prayers.

Building Kids Faith Series

God

9 We talk with God through prayer.

- We can have a relationship with God.
- Relationships depend on good communications.
- We talk with God through prayer.

DID YOU KNOW?

Of all of the world's religions, Christianity is the only one where friendship with God is possible.

What do YOU think?

Who is your best friend?

What makes you friends? The Creator of the universe wants to be your friend; are you interested?

How could anyone tell if you were God's friend?

Challenge

Try to spend as much time with God in one week as you do with your best friend in one day.

God

9 We talk with God through prayer.

TALK about it

Describe some of the things you do or would never do with your best friend.

Think About It

Take a look at John 15:9–17. There may be no greater passage in the Bible to describe the kind of relationship God wants to have with us. He doesn't want slaves; He doesn't want soldiers, employees, or co-workers. He doesn't want teachers, students, neighbors, or teammates. He wants friends. In fact He said, "Before they call I will answer; while they are still speaking I will hear" (Isaiah 65:24). Do you want to be His friend? Are you willing to do what it takes to have a relationship with God? Spend time with Him. Talk with Him. We can all use a good friend.

Memorize It

Put this verse on your front or back door. Every time you enter or leave, knock on the door and repeat the verse out loud.

Here I am! I stand at the door and knock. If anyone hears my voice and opens the door, I will come in and eat with him, and he with me.
Revelation 3:20

Pray About It

Make time to spend with God by yourself and together as a family. Tell Him about your day—the fun and the bad stuff. Talk to Him like a friend.

God

10 God wants us to praise and worship Him.

- Worship is all about God and not about us.
- God wants us to praise and worship Him.
- We worship God by giving Him our whole life and by loving others.

What do YOU think?

Do you have a favorite sports team or music group? How do you show that you really like them? Do your friends know you are a fan? What are some ways your friends know that you think God is cool? What are ways you could show God you think He is cool? All of these ideas are called worship. Do you worship God?

DID YOU KNOW?

The longest book in the Bible is Psalms; its 150 chapters are filled with words of prayer, praise, and worship.

Challenge

Think of ways you can show God that you are His biggest fan. Come up with a new idea every day.

God

10 God wants us to praise and worship Him.

TALK about it

Who is the biggest sports fan you know? Who is the biggest God fan?

Think About It

We worship all the time. Just watch sports fans. We worship by cheering, praising, and shouting. We worship by spending time and money on things we love. Romans 12:1 tells us to offer our body as "a living sacrifice." That means we need to cheer for God by the way we think, the way we spend, and the way we live. Worship goes far beyond church. Your friends are able to tell if you are a sports fan. They should also be able to tell if you are a fan of God. Deuteronomy 6:6–7 says, "These commandments that I give you today are to be upon your hearts. Impress them upon your children. Talk about them when you sit at home and when you walk along the road, when you lie down and when you get up." We need to live in such a way that everyone who sees us will know that we really believe in Jesus. Do your friends know you are a fan of God?

Memorize It

Have each family member make up a tune and sing this psalm, or put the words to a tune you know. Sing it as part of your bedtime prayer this week.

Worship the LORD with gladness; come before him with joyful songs.
Psalm 100:2

Pray About It

Write a poem, song, or short story about God and read it to the family. You can do this as individuals or a family.

Scripture

11 The Bible is God's Word.

- God speaks to us through the Bible.
- The Bible is God's Word because it points to Jesus.
- The written Word helps us spread the good news to everyone.

What do YOU think?

In the space below write a letter to your friends and tell them one very important thing they need to know.

DID YOU KNOW?

The entire book of Jonah covers only about 1 month of history, but 2 Chronicles covers almost 400 years!

How many important things did you think of? How did you decide what to write down and what to leave out?

Challenge

This week take the time to let your friends and family know that you really care about them. Use a letter, e-mail, or phone call.

Scripture

Family Devotions

12 The Bible shows us who God is and what He has done.

TALK about it

What would you do to let someone know as much about you as possible?

Think About It

The best movies ever made and the best books ever written may have changed people. But no book in the history of the world has changed entire countries. The Bible has made a difference for good for the whole world. Take a look at Exodus 3:7–10. While this true story is about God rescuing the Hebrews from Egypt, a larger story is also told in these verses. We have a God who hears, who cares, and who acts on our behalf. This story is just one of hundreds throughout the Bible that shows us the character of God and His concern for His people. He loves us and desires to be in a relationship with us. The Bible shows us who God is and what He has done. And if we read it we learn that God is good, God is great, and He can be trusted.

Memorize It

Have each person write the verse on a piece of paper and hide it from the others. When each piece is found shout the verse out loud.

We will not hide them from their children; we will tell the next generation the praiseworthy deeds of the LORD, his power, and the wonders he has done. Psalm 78:4

Pray About It

Have each person tell an Old Testament story. Discover different ways God shows His love. Spend time thanking God for all the different ways He shows His love to us.

Building Kids FAITH Series

Scripture

 13 **God's Word never changes.**

- God's revelation in written word has been passed down to us.
- When God's Word is hidden in our heart, it endures; it never changes.
- We are responsible for passing on words of life that we read in the Bible to others.

DID YOU KNOW?

Genesis means "beginnings." The last word in the Bible is "Amen!"

What do YOU think?

Make a list of the most trustworthy people you know.

What makes these people trustworthy? What causes you to loose your trust in another person? What would you do to make yourself more trustworthy and dependable?

Challenge

As you read your Bible, keep track of things that would be valuable to share with others. Find time to share those things with others.

Scripture

13 God's Word never changes.

TALK about it

Talk about people who have disappointed you because they said one thing but then did something else.

Think About It

Dependability, reliability, permanence—these are words that help us feel secure. Not many people, places, or things remain steady for the long haul. But God does, and His Word is rock solid.

Take a look at Revelation 1:8. "'I am the Alpha and the Omega,' says the Lord God, 'who is, and who was, and who is to come, the Almighty.'" What a refreshing, encouraging promise! With all the inconsistent leaders we have seen, it's good to know there is a Power that won't let you down. Jesus said in the Gospel of John that the Word of God was there before the beginning. He will be there after the ending. He never changes; the Word of God never changes. Do you know anyone who needs the dependability, reliability, and permanence that comes from a relationship with God and His Word? "Jesus Christ is the same yesterday and today and forever" (Hebrews 13:8).

Memorize It

Have a parent think of something alive, say how long it lives, and then recite the verse. Have the next person think of something that lives a little longer, and repeat the whole process.

Heaven and earth may pass away, but my words will never pass away. Matthew 24:35

Pray About It

Think of things that change frequently and things that don't ever seem to change. Remember God's love, mercy, grace, and power never change. Thank Him that He never changes.

Scripture

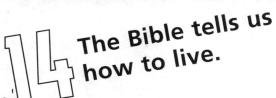 **14 The Bible tells us how to live.**

- **The Bible is a guide for life.**
- **The Old and New Testaments provide teaching for our lives.**
- **Scripture also gives us examples of how other faithful people lived.**
- **The Bible tells us how to live.**

DID YOU KNOW?

The book of Genesis is quoted 260 times in the New Testament.

What do YOU think?

Ask five people who their Bible heroes are. Ask them why they chose those heroes.

Challenge

Find the story of your favorite Bible hero and read it carefully. Note the things you can learn, and ask God to help you apply them.

Building Faith Kids Series

Scripture

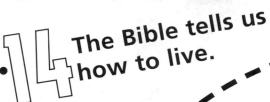

14 The Bible tells us how to live.

TALK about it

Find an owner's manual for a television. How does this manual help you use and enjoy the television?

Think About It

Look at this week's memory verse. It says "All Scripture is God-breathed . . ." Every time you pick up your Bible, ask yourself these questions: What does this passage tell me about God? What does this passage tell me about myself? What am I going to do about it? When we read the Bible simply to be obedient, we will usually learn something. God will not let the time be wasted. When we read it for the right reasons, God will bless the time. When you pick up your Bible, ask the three questions above and you will learn something every time. Our memory verse ends with "so that the man of God may be thoroughly equipped for every good work." Learning God's Word will always be useful. It may not be immediate, but it will be useful. Read 2 Timothy 3:16–17 and ask those questions.

Memorize It

Each night at dinner talk about one of the following: God-breathed; teaching; rebuking; correcting; training; righteousness; equipped. After talking about the words, try to say the verse from memory.

All Scripture is God-breathed and is useful for teaching, rebuking, correcting and training in righteousness, so that the man of God may be thoroughly equipped for every good work.
2 Timothy 3:16–17

Pray About It

Every day read a different chapter in the book of Proverbs. List things that can help you live a better life. Pray that God will help you do these things.

Self

 15 I am created in the image of God.

- We are created in the image of God.
- God's image includes His character and qualities.
- We are the only part of God's creation that He made in His image.

 **What do YOU think?**

Draw a picture of yourself or write a paragraph describing what you look like.

DID YOU KNOW?

Original manuscripts of the Bible weren't written on paper. Instead they were written on papyrus, parchment, or vellum.

In what ways are you similar or different from God the Father? Now describe your personality traits and your character; in other words, describe the kind of person you are.

Challenge

Watch people this week, looking for people acting like God might act in similar situations. What can you learn about God by watching people?

 Building Kids Faith Series

Self

15 I am created in the image of God.

TALK about it

Stand in front of a mirror with your family and point out all the ways that you look similar.

Think About It

When we see a baby animal we can usually tell what its parents look like. Fur color may be different, but kittens don't have dog parents and canaries don't have baby fish. People are a lot like that too. Most kids share some similar characteristics with their parents. A long or short nose, red hair, and blue eyes are all characteristics that are inherited.

We also inherit characteristics from our Heavenly Father. "This is the written account of Adam's line. When God created man, he made him in the likeness of God" (Genesis 5:1). Our soul is marked with the design and imagination of the Creator. When we think about that we should rejoice. We are made in God's image, which means we have worth, value, and purpose. Because we are created by God we can know that we are not a mistake. Celebrate your uniqueness and heritage.

Memorize It

Write this verse on a Post-it© and stick it on every mirror in the house. Whenever you look in the mirror recite the verse. Say it from memory as soon as you can.

So God created man in his own image, in the image of God he created him; male and female he created them.
Genesis 1:27

Pray About It

Have everyone make a Playdoh© person. How is it like or unlike a real person? How are you like or unlike God? Thank Him for making us in His image.

Self

16 I am unique and valuable to God.

- Because we are made in God's image, we are very valuable to Him.

- God is our creator, and He is interested in each one of our lives.

- Because of our unique worth, God has given us special responsibilities.

What do YOU think?

How are you different from everyone else on the planet? What things do you do well? What are some things for which people compliment you? What do you really enjoy doing? How can you use that to serve God?

DID YOU KNOW?

When King David rescued the Ark of the Covenant, the entire army stopped every six steps and worshipped.

Challenge

Make a list of your spiritual gifts. Try to use your gifts to serve others every day this week.

Building Kids FAITH Series

Self

16 I am unique and valuable to God.

TALK about it

Take turns telling each other something that makes them special and different from everyone else.

Think About It

Did you ever stop to think that we are more unique than a snowflake? Everyone marvels that each little piece of frozen water is different. But it is, after all, just water. Humans are unique in billions of different ways. And, unlike snowflakes, we can use our differences to serve others and to serve God. Ephesians 2:10 says, "For we are God's workmanship, created in Christ Jesus to do good works, which God prepared in advance for us to do." Think about that. God made us unique, and before we were even created He was already creating ways in which we can serve Him! How exciting! Ephesians 1:4 says that God chose us before the world was made. With words like that we should never feel useless or inferior. We should never put ourselves or others down. We are of extreme value to God and to God's kingdom. He has great plans for us. We should do whatever we can to put our talent to His work.

Memorize It

Have family members point out ways they are different from each other. After each example, recite the verse as a family.

· · · · · · · · · · · · · · · ·

I praise you because I am fearfully and wonderfully made; your works are wonderful, I know that full well.
Psalm 139:14

Pray About It

Each day search the house for one valuable thing. Remind each other that you are worth more than the most valuable thing you can find, and thank God.

Self

 I am responsible for my choices.

- I am responsible for my choices.
- God has given us both the ability and the accountability of choice.
- We honor God by obeying Him and thinking of others.

 **What do YOU think?**

 **DID YOU KNOW?**

King Solomon spoke three thousand proverbs. Many of his proverbs are recorded in the book of Proverbs.

Where do you turn when you need advice?

What are the things for which you seek advice?

Are there people you know you would never go to for advice? Why do you avoid those people?

Do you ever blame others for your choices? Why or why not?

 **Challenge**

Every day for the next month read one chapter in the book of Proverbs, a book all about making wise choices.

Self

17 I am responsible for my choices.

Think About It

In the Book of Joshua, the people made a series of wise and unwise choices. God allowed them to make mistakes and make right decisions. He even told them in advance the consequences of choosing correctly or incorrectly. At the very end of the book, when Joshua had finished the task God called him to do, he had one final message for the people. Joshua 24:14–15 says, "Now fear the LORD and serve him with all faithfulness . . . But if serving the LORD seems undesirable to you, then choose for yourselves this day whom you will serve, whether the gods your forefathers served beyond the River, or the gods of the Amorites in whose land you are living. But as for me and my household, we will serve the LORD." We face the same decision. We can choose to follow God or not. The wise choice is to daily make the decision to follow God. Remember that when it is time to make any kind of decision, pray about it, weigh the consequences, and choose wisely.

TALK about it

People often blame others for their mistakes. How does this make you feel? Do you like being around those people?

Memorize It

Make a batch of cookies. When the timer goes off, say, "This is how we know the cookies are ready. How do we know we love the children of God?" Respond by saying the verse.

This is how we know we love the children of God: by loving God and carrying out his commands.
1 John 5:2

Pray About It

Everyone write down one way you want to obey God better. Pray to make good choices. Thank God for His help. Make a new list each day.

Self

18 God wants my thoughts and actions to be pure.

- God created everything good, beautiful, and noble.
- God wants your thoughts and actions to be pure.
- The good, beautiful, and noble things that enter our lives will be reflected in our relationship with God and others.

What do YOU think?

Think about two or three people you admire the most. What are some of the things that you admire about them? What can you do to become the kind of person others admire?

DID YOU KNOW?

The longest chapter in the Bible is Psalm 119, and the shortest is Psalm 117.

Challenge

Read and meditate on Philippians 4:8. Every day take a different word and ask yourself, "How can I be more like this today?"

Building Kids FAITH Series

Self

Family
Devotions

18 God wants my thoughts and actions to be pure.

TALK about it

What do pure thoughts sound like? What about pure actions? How can we look and sound more like that?

Think About It

Would you ever consider adding a little dirt to your brownie recipe? The color is right, even the texture would mix right in with the rest of the ingredients. But you wouldn't think of adding something so disgusting to your brownies. Double yuck! What about your life and your words? Do you ever add just a little dirt to your talk? Do you include a little nastiness, just a small, bad thought thrown in here or there? Just as adding dirt to your brownies would ruin the whole batch, adding impure thoughts and actions can ruin your life. Read and meditate on Philippians 4:8. As you fill your mind with pleasant words, thoughts, and actions, there will be less and less room in your life for bad thoughts. Remember, "He chose us in him before the creation of the world to be holy and blameless in his sight" (Ephesians 1:4).

Memorize It

On day one list the eight key words and talk about their meaning. Memorize the key words and fill in the rest of the verse for the rest of the week.

Finally, brothers, whatever is true, whatever is noble, whatever is right, whatever is pure, whatever is lovely, whatever is admirable—if anything is excellent or praiseworthy— think about such things. Philippians 4:8

Pray About It

Talk about people and things that help you to please God and the people or things that are not pleasing to God. Pray for wisdom to make the right choices.

Building Kids Faith Series

Self

19 I can use my talents and abilities to please God.

- God has given each of us many different talents and abilities.

- I can use my talents and abilities to please God.

- Everything we say or do should glorify and please God.

What do YOU think?

What are your gifts and talents? What do you do really well?

DID YOU KNOW?

In 1947 while throwing rocks, a boy accidentally found 1,900-year-old Bible manuscripts called The Dead Sea Scrolls.

How would your friends like to be more like you?

What good things do you really enjoy doing?

In what ways are you most like Jesus?

Challenge

Read I Peter 4:8–11 each day. Ask God for the strength and ability to put these words into action this week.

Building Kids FAITH Series

Self

19

I can use my talents and abilities to please God.

TALK about it

Make a list of the strengths, talents and gifts of everyone in your family.

Think About It

Check out Ephesians 2:10, and then look at this week's memory verse again. Many kids and adults wonder why they were made. Many feel like they are not good at anything and some even feel they are a bother or a burden to others. When you feel this way, remind yourself of these two passages and other ones that tell us that we were made on purpose for a purpose. The reason we are here is to bring glory to God. The most fun and rewarding thing we can do is discover our gifts and talents and use them for God. When we serve God with our abilities, we are like a championship team where everyone is playing their part to make the whole team look good. God created everyone with special abilities that are unique to that person.

Memorize It

Each evening, take turns reading sections of the verse. Each person may have more than one section. Repeat the verse in order several times, switching sections each evening.

And whatever you do, whether in word or deed, do it all in the name of the Lord Jesus, giving thanks to God the Father through him. Colossians 3:17

Pray About It

Every day focus on one family member, pointing out that person's spiritual gifts and talents. Pray for that family member and the use of those talents.

Jesus

20 Jesus is the Son of God.

- Jesus is the Son of God.
- God sent His Son, Jesus, to earth.
- We know God because we have Jesus.

DID YOU KNOW?

The Old Testament contains 300 prophesies about Jesus. (A prophecy is a prediction made by someone who speaks for God.)

What do YOU think?

Imagine trying to rescue an animal from danger. Not only is the animal in danger, but it is also afraid of you. What would you do? How would you help?

How would you let the animal know that it could trust you and that you were there to help?

How is this like or unlike what God did for us when He sent Jesus to earth?

Challenge

Read John 1:1–14. Take your time, reading two or three verses each day. Then write down the things you discover about Jesus.

Jesus

20 Jesus is the Son of God.

Think About It

God became man. There is no question that this is probably the biggest mystery on earth. How can He be both God and man? It is a mystery we will probably never fully understand on earth. It's okay to have questions. That is where faith and trust come in. When we look at all we do know about God, we can trust Him completely and know His Word is true. This is a good time to look at John 3:16. What do we know about God? He loves us. What did He do? He sent us Jesus. Why did He send Jesus? He sent Jesus to save us and give us eternal life.

Everything we see in Jesus represents God the Father. We understand God and His ways better by studying Jesus. Look at Matthew 16:12–20. Note that even the disciples that walked with Jesus everyday didn't completely understand, but they learned to trust. As you try to understand Jesus, remember that the most important thing is to trust Him and not just to understand Him.

TALK about it

Talk about Jesus and what confuses you about Him. Remember that some things can never be completely understood about God.

Memorize It

Have someone write the verse and draw a picture. Have each person say the verse and try to copy the first drawing exactly. Have someone different draw a picture and start the verse each day.

The Son is the radiance of God's glory and the exact representation of his being, sustaining all things by his powerful word. Hebrews 1:3

Pray About It

Make a list of things that happen to children (good and bad). Remind everyone that Jesus probably experienced these things too. Thank God for sending us Jesus.

Jesus

21 **Jesus lived on earth.**

- Jesus came to earth as a human.
- Jesus lived on earth.
- As a human, Jesus experienced life as we experience it.

What do YOU think?

Make a list of everything you did today. Look at the list; how do you think Jesus would act in each of the situations you have written down? Did you do things that Jesus would not do? Would Jesus do some things differently? How? Why do you think Jesus became a human? Write your answer below.

DID YOU KNOW?

WHENTHENEWTESTAMENTWASORIGINALLYWRITTENTHEREWERENOSPACESBETWEENTHEWORDS. When the New Testament was originally written there were no spaces between the words.

Challenge

This week as you walk to class or to lunch, imagine Jesus walking right beside you. How does your behavior change?

Jesus

 Jesus lived
on earth.

TALK
about it

Have everyone pick a number between one and thirty-three. Discuss what Jesus might have been like at the ages you picked.

Think About It

"You don't understand me" is something most of us have said. We can't say that about Jesus. He lived and moved on earth as a human being. He probably skinned His knee as a young boy, had a runny nose, and maybe He didn't like scrambled eggs either. He went through many, if not all, of the struggles every other boy His age went through. It hurt when people made fun, and it felt good when they cheered. His pain was real. Hebrews 4:15–16 says, "For we do not have a high priest who is unable to sympathize with our weaknesses, but we have one who has been tempted in every way, just as we are . . . Let us then approach the throne of grace with confidence, so that we may receive mercy and find grace to help us in our time of need." How are you feeling today? He understands. Is school really tough right now? He understands. Is work hard? God understands. Is everything going great? He understands that too. He understands, and He cares.

Memorize It

Copy and hide the five parts of this verse. Send children out to find them. When you find all the pieces put them in order and read the verse together out loud.

The Word became flesh and made his dwelling among us. We have seen his glory, the glory of the One and Only, who came from the Father, full of grace and truth.
John 1:14

Pray About It

Talk about what it would be like if Jesus sat next to you at class, work, or home. Thank Jesus for understanding your daily needs.

Jesus

22 Jesus is both God and human.

- Jesus is completely God and completely human.
- When Jesus came to earth, He did not lose His divinity but took on humanity.
- Jesus was called "Emmanuel," which means "God with us."

What do YOU think?

If you were the most powerful person on earth how would you use your power for good? How would you be tempted to use your power, just for yourself or for evil purposes?

DID YOU KNOW?

When Jesus was on earth people who were sick were not allowed to go to church.

Challenge

When you face tough situations this week, remind yourself that "God is with us." When things are going great remember, "God is with us."

Jesus

 22 Jesus is both God and human.

TALK
about it

What is the best thing about God always being with us? What is the worst thing about it?

Think About It

Read Philippians 2:6–11. The early church had no questions about who Jesus was. Many modern scholars try to tell us that Jesus never taught that He was God and that even early Christians didn't believe He was God, but this passage shows us beyond a doubt that the early church understood who Jesus was. Verses six and seven cannot be understood any other way. Jesus was God. His nature, what He was made of, was God. Not like God, not partially God, but 100% God. This passage was written only a few years after Jesus' death and resurrection. It may be one of the very first Christian songs. It was the core and the center of the faith of the early church. Jesus was 100% human and 100% God. Jesus was very clear when He said, "I and the Father are one" (John 10:30) and "anyone who has seen me has seen the Father" (John 14:9). He was fully human and fully God.

Memorize It

This verse will be best remembered if everyone understands all of the key words, so take time to discuss words like Deity, fullness, power and authority. Then start reciting.

For in Christ all the fullness of the Deity lives in bodily form, and you have been given fullness in Christ, who is the head over every power and authority.
Colossians 2:9–10

Pray About It

List happy things your family does together and list unhappy or scary times. Talk about where God was when those things happened. Thank God for always being with you.

Jesus

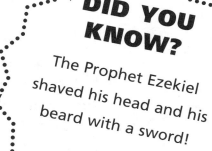

23 **Jesus was tempted but did not sin.**

- As a human, Jesus had desires like us.
- Jesus was tempted but did not sin.
- Though we are tempted, we can choose not to sin.

What do YOU think?

What things are most tempting for you?

What things are most likely to cause you to make unwise choices?

What places are you most likely to get into trouble? When are you more likely to do the wrong thing?

When are you most likely to make a wise choice? When it is easy to do the right thing?

DID YOU KNOW?

The Prophet Ezekiel shaved his head and his beard with a sword!

Challenge

Make a list of the places and things you should avoid. Carry it with you and remind yourself that you can choose not to sin.

Jesus

23 Jesus was tempted but did not sin.

TALK about it

Have everyone list places where people would probably choose to sin and places where people would choose not to sin.

Think About It

Read the story of Jesus' temptation in Luke 4:1–13. Remember that Jesus was a human, and He faced temptations. When you read this passage you will see that Jesus used the same thing to fight temptations that you and I can use—the Bible. Every time the Devil offered a temptation, Jesus used a passage from the Old Testament to fight temptation. We not only have the Old Testament, but we have the New Testament too. "Because he himself suffered when he was tempted, he is able to help those who are being tempted" (Hebrews 2:18). The two best tools to fight temptation are the Bible and prayer. Reading and memorizing parts of the Bible will give us the words we need to make the right choice and not sin, and talking to Jesus will give us the strength we need to choose wisely and to make the right decision.

Memorize It

Choose someone to recite the verse until they get stuck. Have the next person start over and recite until faltering. Continue until someone finishes it without mistakes.

For we do not have a high priest who is unable to sympathize with our weakness, but we have one who has been tempted in every way, just as we are—yet was without sin.
Hebrews 4:15

Pray About It

Make a list of the main places you will go throughout the week. Ask God to help you always make the right choice, no matter where you are.

Jesus

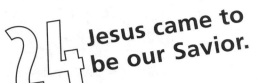 **Jesus came to be our Savior.**

- The Son, Jesus Christ, had a special purpose in coming to earth.
- Jesus came to be our Savior.
- Jesus is our Savior because of what He did.

What do YOU think?

Make a list or draw a picture of bad things in the world.

Make a list or draw a picture of good things.

What is the best thing?

DID YOU KNOW?

God changed Jacob's name to Israel, which means "struggles with God." His descendants (his children and grandchildren) were called Israelites.

Challenge

This week spend time thinking about the last week of Jesus' life. Read Luke 22, 23, and 24 to remember better what Jesus did for you.

Jesus

24 Jesus came to be our Savior.

TALK about it

Discuss the parts of your life that are out of your control. Who can do something about those things?

Think About It

When it comes to the issue of sin, we need God's help. We can choose not to sin, but often we don't. We don't have the ability to live without sinning for our entire life, and we cannot pay the price for our sin. We need someone to pay for it for us. We need Jesus. Romans 5:6–8 tells the story. We need help. At exactly the right moment Jesus came. He paid the price we cannot pay on our own. We may ask, "Why did Jesus come?" The answer is very clear. He came to save us. Jesus said, "I have come into the world as a light, so that no one who believes in me should stay in darkness" (John 12:46). He came to save us from our sins. Do you want His salvation?

Memorize It

Have one family member ask another, "Why did God send His Son into the world?" For an answer recite the verse. Repeat the process until everyone has had a chance to say the verse.

. . . .

For God did not send his Son into the world to condemn the world, but to save the world through him.
John 3:17

Pray About It

Talk about the purpose of objects that are around the room. Talk about the purpose of Jesus coming to Earth. Spend a few minutes quietly thanking God for Jesus' life.

Jesus

25 Jesus died on the cross.

- Jesus' mission to be our Savior included His own suffering and death.
- Jesus' suffering occurred throughout His life.
- Jesus ultimately suffered death on the cross.

What do YOU think?

When was the last time you thanked God for the gift of Jesus? Write God a thank you note.

DID YOU KNOW?

A parable is a story about something common representing something unknown. Jesus used over 40 different parables during His ministry.

Challenge

Find a small cross. Carry it in your pocket everywhere you go. Whenever you reach into your pocket remember what Jesus did for you.

Jesus

 **25** Jesus died on the cross.

 **TALK about it**

What is the nicest thing anyone has ever done for you? (Not counting what Jesus did.)

Think About It

Read the account of Jesus' crucifixion in Matthew 27:32–56. Our mission is to please and glorify God with our life. Jesus' mission was to please and glorify God with His death. The pain He suffered, the humiliation He felt, and the death He experienced was the reason He came to earth. The people for whom He died were you and me. When you think you are not valuable, remember Jesus thought enough of you to die for you. He wants to be part of your life, and He was willing to pay any price for that friendship. When you think you are alone and friendless, remember His gift. Wherever you go and whatever you do, remember His gift. "Let us fix our eyes on Jesus, the author and perfector of our faith, who for the joy set before him endured the cross, scorning its shame, and sat down at the right hand of the throne of God" (Hebrews 12:2).

Memorize It

Talk about one section of the verse at a time, making sure everyone understands it. Talk about one section each night for three nights, then work on all three sections for three nights.

And being found in appearance as a man, he humbled himself and became obedient to death— even death on a cross! Philippians 2:8

Pray About It

Use this week's memory verse as your prayer focus. Make your prayer time this week free from asking for things; simply go to God with grateful hearts.

Jesus

 26 **God raised Jesus from the dead.**

- After Jesus was crucified, His body was laid in a tomb for three days.

- God raised Jesus from the dead.

- After Jesus was resurrected, the disciples met with Him for forty days and witnessed His ascension to heaven.

What do YOU think?

Draw a picture or write a story about a big victory celebration. What are the people saying and doing? Why are they happy? How long will the happiness last?

Now think about the celebration in heaven when Jesus rose from the dead. What do you think that party was like?

DID YOU KNOW?

Zechariah and Isaiah predicted the way Jesus would die 500–700 years before His birth and before crucifixion had been invented.

Challenge

Every time you feel sad or overwhelmed this week, remember the victory of Jesus over death. Ask God for victory over sadness or problems.

Building Kids Faith Series

Jesus

26 God raised Jesus from the dead.

TALK about it

Talk about the best party you ever attended. Compare it with the celebration when Jesus rose from the dead.

Think About It

Think about the followers of Jesus and how sad they must have been when Jesus died. Then think about how they felt when they heard that He had risen from the dead. At first they must have been really confused; some didn't even believe it. Now think about how they felt as they began to understand what had happened. The power of God was at work right where they were living. They began to understand that Jesus really was God! Read Luke 24 or John 20 to get an understanding of how Jesus' friends felt and responded to His death and resurrection. When we think about this great miracle performed for you and me, we should throw a party! When you feel defeated, remember that Jesus defeated death. Jesus' victory is our victory. Jesus' body spent three days in the ground to fulfill prophesies, and then He rose from the dead. He appeared to His disciples and hundreds of eye witnesses. Then He went to heaven. Hallelujah! Jesus is alive.

Memorize It

As your family prepares for bedtime, say the verse two or three times each evening.

But Christ has indeed been raised from the dead, the firstfruits of those who have fallen asleep.
1 Corinthians 15:20

Pray About It

Read Luke 24, stopping frequently to remember that it happened for you. Be thoughtful and quiet, yet joyful, as you think of the greatest gift of all. Thank God for this gift.

Salvation

27 All people have done wrong.

- Adam and Eve were the first people to sin.
- Sin is not God's intention for us.
- All people have done wrong, or sinned.

What do YOU think?

Think about the nicest people you know. How much do you know about them? Do you suppose they have said, done or thought things that were not nice? How much do people know about you? How many things do you do or think that you hope no one ever finds out about? Write down something you have done or thought that is wrong. Ask God to forgive you. Scribble it out so no one can read it.

DID YOU KNOW?

Early Jewish leaders took the Ten Commandments and developed almost six hundred rules that everyone was supposed to follow.

Challenge

Ask God to remind you every time you sin. When He reminds you, ask for forgiveness, and ask for His help to stop.

Salvation

 27 **All people have done wrong.**

TALK about it

Everyone share one or two things that you are really good at. How close to perfect are you?

Think About It

It's sometimes hard to talk about, but we all sin. Everyone who ever lived since the first man and woman has sinned. Sometimes we start to compare one person to another person. I may be mean once in a while, but I'm not as bad as that person over there. The problem with that is we are comparing ourselves to people. God says we need to compare our life to His. When we do, we all fall short because we all need a Savior. Romans 3:23 says, "For all have sinned and fall short of the glory of God." Everyone has sinned, without exception. Jesus was the only person who lived a perfect life. Not even Noah, Mary, Joseph, Moses, Joshua or David. Every person who has walked the face of the earth, except Jesus, has sinned. Sin separates us from God. That is why we need Jesus. How have you sinned? Ask God to forgive you.

Memorize It

Each day ask your child to do a task that is impossible for them to do. After they have fallen short in their attempt, read the verse and have them recite it back to you.

. . . .

For all have sinned and fall short of the glory of God. Romans 3:23

Pray About It

Tell each other about something you asked God to forgive. As you pray, remind everyone that once you ask God for forgiveness, that sin is forgiven forever.

Salvation

28 Sin separates people from God.

- Sin is bad because it separates us from God.
- Sin makes us less than what God made us to be.
- God wants us to have a good relationship with Him because He knows it's best for us.

What do YOU think?

Have you ever had a best friend and lost that friendship because of something you did? Or do you know anyone who has lost their best friend because of what one of them did? You probably know someone who has gotten a divorce. Write a story of something that broke a friendship.

When friends break up or marriages fall apart, how does it feel? How must God feel when we sin?

DID YOU KNOW?

The words "grace" and "mercy" appear in the Bible twice as often as the words "punish" or "punishment."

Challenge

Find someone this week that you have hurt with your words or actions and ask for their forgiveness. Ask if you can be friends again.

Salvation

28 Sin separates people from God.

TALK about it

What are some of the bad things that happen when people treat others badly?

Think About It

The consequence of sin is death (Romans 6:23)—permanent separation from God. We fall short of the glory of God. We cannot reach God in our sinfulness, which means we cannot get to heaven with our own good deeds. It doesn't matter what anyone else in the world has done or will do; what matters is you. Your sin separates you from God. God chose to let us have free will (the right to decide what we want to do), and we made the wrong choice. We continue to make wrong choices. We continue to sin. Every sin, even ones we call little tiny sins, moves us away from God. Sin separates us from God. We need a Savior. We need to be saved from our sins. Jesus is the Savior. How are you separated from God?

Memorize It

Put this verse on the inside of everyone's bedroom door. Have everyone read it to themselves when they get up in the morning and then recite it to whomever they eat breakfast with.

No one who lives in him keeps on sinning. No one who continues to sin has either seen him or knows him.
1 John 3:6

Pray About It

Give examples of sins, stepping away from each other as you do. Turn around, walk back, saying, "God forgives us when we ask." Thank God for forgiveness.

Salvation

29 God loves us even though we have sinned.

- God wants to be in relationship with us because He created us.

- Our separation from God does not diminish His love for us.

- God loves us even though we have sinned.

DID YOU KNOW?

Genesis makes predictions about Jesus (Genesis 3:15). From start to finish the Bible is God's plan of salvation.

What do YOU think?

Have you ever had someone who really wanted to be your friend and you weren't sure why? Have you ever wanted someone to be your friend and you would do almost anything to be their friend?

Write the names of your friends.

Now write the names of people you would like to be your friends.

Think about what you can do to make a new friend.

Challenge

Send a note to as many friends as you can, thanking them for being your friend, even if they haven't always been nice to you.

Salvation

 29 God loves us even though we have sinned.

TALK about it

What is a friend? Why should someone want to be your friend? Why would you want to be someone's friend?

Think About It

"But God demonstrates his own love for us in this: While we were still sinners, Christ died for us" (Romans 5:8). God doesn't need friends the way we do. God doesn't need anything. But He is so full of love that He doesn't want us to be lost and separated from Him. As hard as it is to believe, God does not love us any less when we sin. When someone treats us badly, we respond by being hurt and then by choosing to forgive or not to forgive. We even choose whether or not we will continue to be friends. God doesn't respond that way. He always responds in love. He is always willing and ready to take us back. Read the story of the father and son in Luke 15:11–32. What picture does this story show of God?

Memorize It

Each evening, give one person an opportunity to demonstrate how to do something. Afterwards recite the verse together and talk about what makes a good demonstration.

. . . .

But God demonstrated his own love for us in this: While we were yet still sinners, Christ died for us.
Romans 5:8

Pray About It

Talk about salvation this week. Pray together for wisdom and the right words to say to your kids. Pray with your kids and give them a chance to accept Christ.

Salvation

30 God sent His Son to forgive sins.

- God showed the extent of His love by sending His Son to earth.
- Through Jesus, God provided a way for us to enter into a relationship with Him.
- God sent His Son to forgive our sins.

What do YOU think?

How often have you gotten something better than you deserved?

Have you ever expected to be punished for something but were shown mercy instead? How did it make you feel?

How often, and in what ways, do you show mercy?

DID YOU KNOW?

If you are a Christian, your name is written down in heaven (Luke 10:20 and Revelation 21:27).

Challenge

Try to show grace to everyone this week, especially if they don't deserve it. Remember the grace God has shown to you.

Salvation

30 God sent His Son to forgive sins.

TALK about it

When someone you love forgives you, how do you feel? How do you feel when you forgive someone you love?

Think About It

Receiving forgiveness is probably one of the very best feelings we can have. When we talk and think about the life of Christ and His death, we should have that kind of good feeling. Jesus died to show us forgiveness. Read Romans 3:22–26. Righteousness is a big word with a big meaning. Righteousness from God means that God has declared that we are not guilty for the sins we have committed. This righteousness comes from Jesus. He took the punishment we deserve. In taking our punishment we have been set free from sin and adopted into God's family. God's mercy, grace, and justice are so great that He not only forgives us and takes us back as friends; He adopts us into His family.

Memorize It

For a change of pace, work on the verse for two days. Then for two days take turns saying Bible passages and seeing who can find them the fastest. Finish the week reviewing the verse.

And we have seen and testify that the Father has sent his Son to be the Savior of the World.
1 John 4:14

Pray About It

Think about things we do that displease God. Ask for forgiveness and thank God for forgiveness. Have a quiet, thankful heart a few minutes every day this week.

Salvation

 31 Jesus died to forgive my sin.

- Because God loves us, He provided atonement for our sins.
- Jesus died to forgive our sins.
- Jesus is the bridge between us and God.

What do YOU think?

Did you ever do anything that was really hard and needed someone to help you? How did those experiences make you feel? Draw a picture of you getting help from someone else.

DID YOU KNOW?

The Bible was written by more than 40 people; rich, poor, young, old, rulers, peasants, educated, and uneducated; but God is the only author!

Challenge

Take as many opportunities as you can to help someone do something that they could not do without your help.

Salvation

 31 Jesus died to forgive my sin.

TALK about it

Talk about a time when someone did something extra nice for you and how it made you feel.

Think About It

Sometimes we want to solve our own problems without any help. Usually when we feel like that it's because we are a little ashamed that we can't do it ourselves, but there are some things we just can't do by ourselves. There are other times when we welcome all the help we can get. When our car is stuck in the snow we never say, "No, I'll just wait until spring." We say, "Thank you!" Jesus provides the help we need to be right with God. Not only is this help nice, but it is necessary. There is no way out except with the help of Jesus.

Thank God He has provided the way out. "I write to you, dear children, because your sins have been forgiven on account of his name" (1 John 2:12).

Memorize It

Show each other a scar on your skin. As you point out each "wound," recite the verse. Look for scars on furniture, walls, trees, etc. Whenever you find a scar recite the verse.

He himself bore our sins in his body on the tree, so that we might die to sins and live for righteousness; by his wounds you have been healed.
1 Peter 2:24

Pray About It

Gather together some building blocks. Build a bridge and talk about what bridges are for. Thank God that Jesus was our bridge to God.

Salvation

 32 God forgives those who believe in Jesus.

- Our relationship with God begins when we confess our sins.

- We should ask God for forgiveness, which He freely gives.

- God forgives those who believe in Jesus.

What do YOU think?

Is it hard for you to admit you are wrong? Is it hard to ask someone to forgive you? What are some of the reasons it is hard for some people to ask for forgiveness?

Is it hard to give forgiveness? Why or why not?

How are giving forgiveness and receiving forgiveness different? How are they similar?

DID YOU KNOW?

The longest book in the New Testament is Luke; chapter 1 of Luke is the longest chapter in the New Testament.

Challenge

Practice being forgiven. Go quickly when you do wrong and ask for forgiveness. Practice forgiveness. When someone hurts you remember the forgiveness you have received.

Salvation

32 God forgives those who believe in Jesus.

TALK about it

Have you ever said, "I'll forgive you, but not right away?" How is that like or unlike God's forgiveness?

Think About It

Relationships that have been damaged do not usually heal all by themselves. Healing doesn't happen until someone asks for forgiveness. Our relationship with God begins when we confess our sins. "If you confess with your mouth, 'Jesus is Lord,' and believe in your heart that God raised him from the dead, you will be saved. For it is with your heart that you believe and are justified, and it is with your mouth that you confess and are saved" (Romans 10:9–10). God's salvation is instantaneous. It happens the moment you ask. God will forgive anyone who believes in Jesus. He doesn't wait for us to become perfect. He doesn't ask us to give more money, pray more, or do anything else but believe in your heart and confess with your mouth. There is real freedom in this kind of forgiveness. If we look at everything we know about God from His Word and His Son, we can believe that He really will forgive us when we ask. Do you have someone you need to forgive?

Memorize It

Talk about the different things each family member has done wrong in the last month. After each thing mentioned, recite the verse.

All the prophets testify about him that everyone who believes in him receives forgiveness of sins through his name.
Acts 10:43

Pray About It

Ask everyone to remember someone they forgave and someone who forgave them. Thank God for the gift of forgiveness; quietly ask Him to forgive you for your wrongdoings.

Salvation

 33 We are adopted into God's family by faith.

- We are adopted into God's family by faith.
- God is a father and a brother to us.
- When we accept Jesus as our Savior, we can take His name by calling ourselves Christians.

What do YOU think?

Have you ever been picked first to be on a team? Have you ever been picked last? How did you feel?

How does it make you feel to know you'll always be picked first by God?

DID YOU KNOW?

During Bible times the hem of a person's clothes was not a practical fold of the cloth. It was an indication of a person's status and importance. The nicer the hem, the more important the person.

Challenge

Write a letter to God thanking Him for adopting you. Write it as if God were a real father who has chosen to adopt you.

Salvation

33 We are adopted into God's family by faith.

TALK about it

What is faith? How do you experience faith in everyday life?

Think About It

Do you know someone who is adopted? They are a real member of that family. Guess what? We are all adopted. Wow! Check out 1 Peter 2:9–10. "But you are a chosen people, a royal priesthood, a holy nation, a people belonging to God, that you may declare the praises of him who called you out of darkness into his wonderful light. Once you were not a people, but now you are the people of God; once you had not received mercy, but now you have received mercy." When God adopts us, we become princes and princesses in His royal family. So, how does it feel to be adopted?

Memorize It

Bring out a family photo album. As you look at each photo, think about being adopted by God and recite the verse to each other.

In love he predestined us to be adopted as his sons through Jesus Christ, in accordance with his pleasure and will.
Ephesians 1:5

Pray About It

Find online or magazine pictures of orphanages in foreign countries. What must their life be like? Pray that orphans would find loving homes; thank God for adopting us.

Salvation

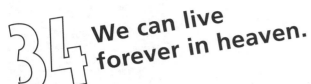

We can live forever in heaven.

- Because we believe in Jesus Christ, we also have the promise of eternal life.
- We can live forever in heaven.
- Jesus is life.

What do YOU think?

Did you ever go on a vacation or do something really special and say, "I wish this could go on forever"? Think about your very favorite place on earth. Draw a picture of you there.

DID YOU KNOW?

The whole Bible can be read aloud in 70 hours.

No matter how great that place is, heaven is better!

Challenge

Spend time thinking about the great places on earth, and thank God for creating them. Try to spend this week with a grateful heart.

Salvation

34 We can live forever in heaven.

TALK about it

If you could travel anywhere on earth where would you choose? Why?

Think About It

Forever is a tough concept to grasp. Talk about fun things you did last year and then talk about events as far back as you can remember. Talk about fun things you did as a child and perhaps something your grandparents did. Remember God's love was present then, as far back as anyone can count, and it will be there as far forward as anyone can imagine. Read Genesis 1. If God gave this much love and thought in creating earth and all that is in it, just imagine what heaven must look like.

Memorize It

Put a copy of this verse on your refrigerator door. Every time someone wants something to eat, they must say the verse to at least one person.

For my Father's will is that everyone who looks to the Son and believes in him shall have eternal life, and I will raise him up on the last day. John 6:40

Pray About It

Pray for people you know that don't seem to know about God's love. Pray that they will see God and choose to follow. Pray that God will use you to help.

Church

35 The Church is all believers everywhere.

- God's family gathers together to form the Church.
- The Church is all believers everywhere.
- Jesus gave the Church a mission to carry out.

What do YOU think?

Write a list of all the things that come to mind when you think about church. What should it look like? What are the people like? Who is part of the Church? When you do this, don't think just of the church you attend, but the Church throughout the world.

DID YOU KNOW?

Three thousand people were saved the first time the story of Jesus was told after He went back to heaven.

Challenge

Drive around and discover the different churches in your community. Ask people from different churches what their services are like or attend one yourself.

Church

35 The Church is all believers everywhere.

TALK about it

Why do you think there are so many different types of churches?

Think About It

Every church is a little different. Some people wonder why there are so many different churches. The key reason is because there are so many wonderful ways to worship God and so many people for the church to reach. Each church has a different set of spiritual gifts especially designed by God to meet the needs of the people who attend. Read Romans 12:3–8. When each individual church or congregation uses its gifts for God, that small group of people becomes part of the Church. The Church is God's tool for reaching the whole world with the good news of Jesus.

Memorize It

Take this one section at a time, and be patient as you discuss it. Talk about what this passage means and the promise it holds for the future.

And they sang a new song: "You are worthy to take the scroll and to open its seals, because you were slain, and with your blood you purchased men for God from every tribe and language and people and nation. You have made them to be a kingdom and priests to serve our God, and they will reign on the earth." Revelation 5:9–10

Pray About It

Take a family drive to visit area churches. Sit in the parking lot of each church and pray that God will help that church grow and reach people for God.

Church

36 We belong to a local church.

- We belong to a local church.
- The mission of the Church is fulfilled through the local church.
- Local churches gather to pray, celebrate the sacraments, and serve.

What do YOU think?

Are you a member of any clubs, teams, or organizations? Why did you join? Is there one you would like to join? Why?

DID YOU KNOW?

There are 1,260 promises and over 8,000 predictions made in the Bible.

Challenge

Make a list of the benefits you bring to your church. What can you do to better serve your church?

Church

36 We belong to a local church.

Think About It

Meeting together to pray, supporting one another, and participating in the sacraments brings joy and fulfillment. Ecclesiastes 4:12 says, "Though one may be overpowered, two can defend themselves. A cord of three strands is not quickly broken." This passage describes the church. The pooling of money, talent, and resources in the local church can help more people than each church member could working on their own. Take a look at Acts 2:42–47. You will see the church working the way it was intended to function. The church met for fellowship, meals, communion, prayer, and hearing the Word of God. They worked together to meet the needs of people in their church and those in their community, and because of this they were looked upon with favor from the whole community. We as a Church today can have the same impact on our community when we do church the way it was intended.

Memorize It

Put a copy of this verse in every room of your house. Throughout the week, as you enter a room, ask each other, "Where is Jesus?" Then recite the verse together.

. . . .

For where two or three come together in my name, there I am with them.
Matthew 18:20

Pray About It

Make a list of as many people as you can that go to your church. Pray for these people by name and that new people would be drawn to Christ.

Church

31

Baptism represents our new life in Christ.

- Baptism is our initiation into God's family.
- In baptism, we symbolically experience the life, death, and resurrection of Christ.
- A sacrament is an outward symbol of what is happening inside.
- Baptism represents our new life in Christ.

DID YOU KNOW?

Baptism came from a ceremony that goes back to the Passover Feast the Israelites celebrated while preparing to leave Egypt.

What do YOU think?

Write a paragraph describing baptism. Tell what you think baptism is and why you should or should not be baptized. Have you been baptized? Write about your experience. If you haven't been baptized, would you like to? Why would you like to be baptized?

Challenge

Practice being still during prayer so that you can listen to God.

Church

31 Baptism represents our new life in Christ.

TALK about it

Have family members who have been baptized talk about how and why they made the decision to be baptized.

Think About It

Baptism serves several purposes in the church. It symbolizes the death and resurrection of Christ, and it symbolizes our new life in Christ. The Bible says that when someone becomes a Christian they are a new creature; the old life is past and a new life begins. (2 Corinthians 5:17) Baptism symbolizes this new birth. Baptism is also an act of submission to God. Baptism is also a permanent reminder of the grace of God and our decision to be a Christ follower. Finally baptism is a public statement, saying that we identify with Christ and His Church. Think about being baptized and thank God for your new life in Christ.

Memorize It

"Bury" this verse somewhere in the house. Have the family seek and find, bring it back, and recite it. Each day someone new hides it. Hide it in your heart.

We were therefore buried with him through baptism into death in order that, just as Christ was raised from the dead through the glory of the Father, we too may live a new life. Romans 6:4

Pray About It

Talk about what baptism represents. Ask God to guide you as you try to live like "a new creation."

Building Kids Faith Series

Church

38 The Lord's Supper represents Christ's sacrifice.

- We celebrate the Lord's Supper to remember Christ's death on the cross.
- We celebrate the Lord's Supper to thank God for His grace and love for us shown in Jesus Christ.
- The Lord's Supper represents Christ's sacrifice.

What do YOU think?

If Communion is a sacrament of remembrance, what are we supposed to remember? List as many things as you can.

What are the benefits of participating in the Lord's Supper (communion)? Are there any reasons not to take communion?

Challenge

The next time you take The Lord's Supper think about the story of Jesus and remember what He did for you.

Building Kids FAITH Series

Church

38 The Lord's Supper represents Christ's sacrifice.

TALK about it

Tell the story of Jesus from the beginning up to today in your own words.

Think About It

Read the story of the Last Supper in Luke 22:14–20 then read what Paul has to say about it in 1 Corinthians 11:23–34. Communion can be a sacred and special moment, or it can be just something you do every now and then. How can you make it special? Start by thinking of it as something special. Prepare your heart and mind. If you know that Communion will be served, talk about it with your family. Read the passages above and others that discuss the Lord's Supper. If you are harboring bad feelings toward someone, go to them and apologize or forgive them. A clean heart makes Communion much more special. Meditate on the death and resurrection of Christ and have a thankful heart. Communion can be a time of celebration, thanksgiving, and remembrance. It is a time to reaffirm that we are saved, that Jesus died and rose from the dead for us, and that we are part of His forever family.

Memorize It

This is a great verse to repeat at every meal you eat together this week; talk about Christ's sacrifice together.

For whenever you eat this bread and drink this cup, you proclaim the Lord's death until he comes.
1 Corinthians 11:26

Pray About It

Each night read one Gospel account of the Last Supper (Matthew 26, Mark 14, Luke 22, John 13). After you read it, give thanks to God for His great sacrifice.

Building Kids FAITH Series

Church

39 We serve others by helping at church.

- We serve others by helping at church.
- The local church allows us to serve the world.
- We learn to love others by loving other brothers and sisters in Christ.

What do YOU think?

Think about all the people who volunteer at your church. How many can you name? Write down their names and what they do. Are there any jobs that need to be done that no one is doing?

DID YOU KNOW?

In the past 200 years close to five billion Bibles have been made and distributed.

Challenge

Make a list of your spiritual gifts and find a way to use at least one of your gifts at church.

Church

39 We serve others by helping at church.

TALK about it

Make a list of all the things that you could do to help out at church.

Think About It

Can you remember a time when you were so sick you couldn't get out of bed? Did someone come and take care of you, doing everything they could to make you feel better? Who do you think felt better, you or the one giving you care? Did you ever notice the wonderful feeling you get by helping others? This should not be a surprise. When God asks us to do something, He always has our best interest at heart. Serving others is what Christ did, and it is one of the reasons He was so wonderful. Jesus came along and cared for the neediest, the least attractive. This showed the love and compassion of God. When we serve others we are being obedient to God, showing the world God's love and compassion, and receiving a blessing for ourselves. It is how Christ lived His life, and it is the way the church imitates Christ. Do you serve at church? If not, think of something you can do.

Memorize It

Each day, one person should talk about a spiritual gift they have and how they can use it. Recite the verse together.

Each one of us should use whatever gift he has received to serve others, faithfully administering God's grace in its various forms.
1 Peter 4:10

Pray About It

Find a time that your family could go to your church without interrupting things. Walk around your church, stopping to pray for the ministry that happens in those places.

Building Faith Kids Series

Church

41 The church spreads the gospel around the world.

- Jesus commands us to go and make disciples.
- The church spreads the gospel around the world.
- Jesus is the good news.

What do YOU think?

Do you know how to tell someone about Jesus? One way is to share your story. Write out your story of Jesus.

DID YOU KNOW?

Almost half of all Americans are named after someone in the Bible.

Challenge

Practice telling someone the plan of salvation with your parents, then go out and share the Gospel with at least one person this week.

Church

41 The church spreads the gospel around the world.

TALK about it

If our love for God was contagious, would anybody catch it from you?

Think About It

The two most important things Jesus told us to do were to love God and others and to share the good news about Jesus. Check out Luke 10:27 and Matthew 28:19. One of the main jobs of the Church is to tell others about Jesus and His love for us. God only made two ways for people to find out about Jesus—meeting Him in person or having someone tell them about Him. Which category do you fit into? If the story about God's love for you and me is the most important story of all, we need to do whatever we can to help spread the good news. That's what "Gospel" means—good news. One way to spread the good news is by helping your church and its missionaries with your tithes. Another way is to tell others about what Jesus did for you. Another is to live your life like you believe the story is true; live a life that pleases God. What are you doing to spread the Gospel around the world?

Memorize It

Create hand motions for each section of this passage. Put them together and recite the verse with the motions. By the end of the week you may want to put it to music.

Therefore go and make disciples of all nations, baptizing them in the name of the Father and of the Son and of the Holy Spirit.
Matthew 28:19

Pray About It

Get a list of missionaries that your church supports, where they serve, and what they need. Each day pray for a missionary and their needs.

Building Kids Faith Series

Church

42 Christians pray for one another.

- Jesus' prayer is our example of how to pray for others.
- Intercessory prayer is praying for one another.
- Christians pray for one another.

What do YOU think?

How do you feel when you know someone is praying for you? How many reasons can you think of to pray for other people? How many people can you name who could use your prayers right now? Write down their names and pray for them.

DID YOU KNOW?

The Apostle Paul includes a prayer for believers in every one of his letters that we have in the Bible.

Challenge

Make a list of people. Put it where you will see it often. Every time you see it, pray for one person on the list.

Church

42 Christians pray for one another.

TALK about it

Think about a time when someone said a prayer for you. How can you spread that good feeling?

Think About It

Read Matthew 18:19–20 and Matthew 21:21–22. Jesus can fix the world's problems without us. He knows our needs even before we speak, but He has asked us to pray for ourselves and for others. In fact He commands us to pray. Prayer is an act of obedience. Prayer not only helps the people for whom we are praying, but it also helps us. We grow closer to God. We remember where all good things come from. We are reminded that God wants to take care of us. We also grow closer to the people for whom we are praying. It makes the Christian community closer. These are all good reasons to remember to pray for others often. The most important reason is because God asks us to pray. How often do you pray for others?

Memorize It

Tape this verse to your dashboard. Recite it as everyone gets into the car.

Be joyful always; pray continually; give thanks in all circumstances, for this is God's will for you in Christ Jesus. 1 Thessalonians 5:16–18

Pray About It

Make a list of people you care for; write specific prayer needs of those people. Take turns praying for every person listed. Remember that God hears and answers our prayers.

Building Kids FAITH Series

Church

 43 Christians meet together for worship.

- Worship includes preparing our hearts, gathering together with brothers and sisters in Christ, and responding to the Word of God.
- Worship is about God, not us.
- Christians meet together for worship.

What do YOU think?

What is your favorite part of the worship service at church? Why? Draw a picture of you worshipping. What are you doing?

DID YOU KNOW?

The word "apostle" means messenger. Jesus started with 12 disciples who became apostles when Jesus sent them out.

Challenge

Look for times and places where you can worship when you are not at church. Make a quiet time for personal worship every day.

Church

 43 Christians meet together for worship.

TALK about it

What is your favorite part of going to church? Why?

Think About It

When you go to a movie or a sporting event you do certain things to get ready. Even getting ready for school requires both kids and parents to do something. When getting ready for church we prepare our body by taking a bath, brushing our teeth, and putting on clean clothes. How often do we take the time to prepare our heart for worship? There is nothing we do in community with others that is as important as worshiping God. Worship not only acknowledges God, His power, and His worth; it actually prepares us for heaven. Isn't that a cool thought?

What can you do to prepare yourself for worship? Take time to pray. Ask God to show you what He wants you to discover this day. Open your heart so God can show you just how much He loves you.

Memorize It

This verse will be easy to memorize if you talk about the four things they "devoted themselves to," and then talk about what your family is devoted to. How can the two lists become similar?

They devoted themselves to the apostles' teaching and to the fellowship, to the breaking of bread and to prayer.
Acts 2:42

Pray About It

Choose one of the Psalms below each day to read aloud as a family prayer of worship: Psalm 9, 19, 27, 33, 47, 66, 81, 92, 98, 100, 103, or 104.

The Christian Life

44

God sent the Holy Spirit to help us.

- The Holy Spirit is the third person in the Trinity.
- God sent His Holy Spirit to help the Church.
- God sent His Holy Spirit to help us.

DID YOU KNOW?

The Holy Spirit gave the apostles power to transform their world. He is mentioned 90 times in the New Testament.

What do YOU think?

Who would you go to for help with the following things: math, science, soccer, building a house, growing up to be like Jesus? If the world's best expert on those subjects came to your house, what kind of questions would you ask?

What questions do you have for God?

Challenge

This week, keep track of the times you wished for good advice. Remember, the Holy Spirit will guide you in making wise choices.

The Christian Life

Family Devotions

44 God sent the Holy Spirit to help us.

TALK about it

Take turns telling about people you go to for help.

Think About It

Sometimes a tour guide is hired to show you around. A tour guide can give you important information about the site you are visiting. We would say, "Wow, I'm really glad we did that!" Read Luke 12:11–12. The Holy Spirit will teach you at the right time what to say. Jesus promised us the Holy Spirit will always lead us in the right direction. Need words in a tough situation? Ask the Holy Spirit. Need freedom from fear? Ask the Holy Spirit. No matter the situation, it will not be too tough for Him. The power that raised Jesus from the dead is available to all believers; that power is the power of the Holy Spirit. Now that's a guide we can use. What thing in your life do you need a guide for?

Memorize It

Start at the end: address first, then the last three words. Add three words at a time until you have finished. You should know this one forwards and backwards.

But the Counselor, the Holy Spirit, whom the Father will send in my name, will teach you all things and will remind you of everything I have said to you.
John 14:26

Pray About It

Look at a compass. The Holy Spirit can be our compass in life. Read Acts 2:1–13 and ask God for the power to do right and avoid wrong.

The Christian Life

45 The Holy Spirit helps us understand the truth.

- **The Holy Spirit helps us understand the truth.**
- **Jesus is the truth.**
- **The Spirit of God lives in us as we become more Christlike.**

What do YOU think?

Can you tell when some people are lying, bragging, or exaggerating? How can you tell?

What are times when you need help to know the truth? You can pray for the Holy Spirit to help you understand the truth.

DID YOU KNOW?

The book of Job is probably the oldest book in the Bible. It was written 1,500 years before Jesus birth.

Challenge

This week pray for discernment, which is the ability to make wise choices and to tell right from wrong. The Holy Spirit gives discernment.

The Christian Life

Family
Devotions

45 The Holy Spirit helps us understand the truth.

TALK about it

Why is it sometimes hard to tell the truth from a lie?

Think About It

Wisdom. Discernment. Truth. These are all things we wish for our children and for ourselves. We all like to be thought of as honest. People flocked to King Solomon because of his wisdom and discernment. (See 1 Kings 3.) How do we become people with wisdom? Read John 16:13–15. Jesus promised the Holy Spirit as a guide. In fact He will guide us into all truth. A life of wisdom and discernment may not be easy, but it is simple. It means asking for the Holy Spirit's help and then listening to and obeying the truth the Spirit gives. The Holy Spirit will never lead you away from obedience or away from God. Is there something right now you need wisdom for?

Memorize It

Put this verse where everyone will see it often. Recite it out loud for all to hear.

And I will ask the Father, and he will give you another Counselor to be with you forever—the Spirit of truth. The world cannot accept him, because it neither sees him, nor knows him. But you know him, for he lives with you and will be in you. John 14:16–17

Pray About It

For what would you like to receive wisdom? Make a list. Add to the list as the week progresses and pray for each person and each item on the list.

The Christian Life

46 The Holy Spirit helps us obey God.

- We must know and obey God.
- The Holy Spirit helps us obey God.
- Obeying God means loving God and loving others.

What do YOU think?

Write down all the rules you can think of for riding your bike.

DID YOU KNOW?

Though many have tried, not one historical fact from the Bible has been disproved. The Bible is totally reliable.

How many of them do you follow without even thinking about them? How many rules do you have to be reminded to follow? How are parents and adults like or unlike the Holy Spirit?

Challenge

Read Romans 8:1–17 every day this week. Ask the Holy Spirit to guide your reading and to learn what He wants you to learn.

The Christian Life

46 The Holy Spirit helps us obey God.

TALK about it

What is the hardest area for you to be obedient? Why?

Think About It

Certain Native Americans describe the conscience as a sharp triangle spinning inside us. It hurts when we make unwise choices, reminding us to stop and change directions. If we don't stop we eventually wear down the points of the triangle, and it no longer hurts to do wrong. The Holy Spirit on the other hand will remind us to make wise choices. The Spirit of God is not a triangle inside us; it is power right from heaven. Romans 8:6 says, "The mind controlled by the Spirit is life and peace." The more we listen and obey the more guidance we will get. Unlike the Native American triangle, obeying God will always result in new guidance, more wisdom, and a better life. Read Ephesians 3:14–19 and take encouragement from the promises in God's Word. We will grow stronger, not weaker as we rely on the Holy Spirit to guide and direct our life.

Memorize It

Have everyone write the verse out, reading out loud as you write. Turn your paper over and try to write out as much as you can remember. Each day you should see improvement.

But the counselor, the Holy Spirit, whom the Father will send in my name, will teach you all things and will remind you of everything I have said to you.
John 14:26

Pray About It

Go around the house and unplug everything you can. Then ask God to show you how to connect and obey Him. Praise Him for direction as you plug back in.

Building Kids FAITH Series

The Christian Life

 47

The Holy Spirit helps us serve others.

- The Holy Spirit helps us serve others.
- We become more like Jesus as we serve others.
- Serving others helps the Church fulfill its mission.

What do YOU think?

Are there people in your community that really need help? List a few of them. In what ways do they need help?

How can you help, and how can you get others from your church to help?

DID YOU KNOW?

The word *bible* comes from the Latin word for "book." Today it means "special book."

Challenge

Put together a team of kids and work on an outreach project for your community. Have mom or dad help supervise the project.

Building Kids Faith Series

The Christian Life
Family Devotions

 47 **The Holy Spirit helps us serve others.**

TALK about it

Talk about the ickiest jobs to do around the house. Who does them? Why?

Think About It

Jesus showed us servanthood in John 13:1–16. Although what Jesus did was not physically hard, it was definitely awkward for everyone involved! Washing someone else's feet shows them that you do not think you are more important, and it shows them you want to serve them. If we listen to the Holy Spirit, He will guide us to people we should help. The Holy Spirit will help us serve others. Some serving projects are just beyond our ability to do on our own. One of the great things about Christianity is that we don't have to do it on our own. We work best in community with other Christians, and God has promised to give us the Holy Spirit to guide us and give us strength. Is there something you should be doing to serve others?

Memorize It

Choose a shepherd. The shepherd gets to "herd" the family around the house, reading short sections of the verse. The sheep repeat the words. Switch shepherds daily.

Keep watch over yourselves and all the flocks of which the Holy Spirit has made you overseers. Be shepherds of the church of God, which he bought with his own blood. Acts 20:28

Pray About It

Everyone share who would be the hardest for you to serve. Pray for strength and wisdom. God may want you uncomfortable, or He may want you to just keep praying.

The Christian Life

48 We grow stronger by learning God's Word.

- Scripture helps us in our relationship with God.
- We grow stronger by learning God's Word.
- When we learn about Jesus, we have a pattern to follow.

What do YOU think?

Write down all the things you have learned to do in the last 12 months. In what ways are you growing and learning as a Christian? Are you growing more like Jesus? How?

DID YOU KNOW?

2 John is the shortest book in the Bible. It is only thirteen verses long.

Challenge

Review all of the Bible memory verses you have worked on this year. How many can you still say from memory?

Building Kids FAITH Series

The Christian Life

48 We grow stronger by learning God's Word.

Think About It

Each day this week read one of the following passages: Ephesians 1:2–14, Philippians 1:2–11, Colossians 1:2–14, 2 Thessalonians 1:2–12. These are powerful prayers filled with promise. The more of God's Word we get into our lives the more easily we will be able to recognize temptation, and the more easily we will be able to walk away from it. When God's Word is in our hearts, the more readily it will come to our mind. When God's Word comes to our mind, we can use it for our benefit and to help make wise choices. There is no greater source of wisdom in the world than the Bible.

Memorize It

Repeat the verse like you would a conversation with each person taking a sentence. Repeat as much as possible from memory the first day and build on it each following day.

How can a young man keep his way pure? By living according to your word. I seek you with all my heart; do not let me stray from your commands. I have hidden your words in my heart that I might not sin against you.
Psalm 119:11

Pray About It

Pick one of the four passages above to read aloud as your prayer. Talk about them together.

Building Kids Faith Series

The Christian Life

49 **We grow stronger by praying to God.**

- Prayer strengthens our relationship with God.
- Prayer was a source of strength for Jesus.
- We grow stronger by praying for God.

What do YOU think?

Think of a great athlete or musician. What habits do they have that make them play or perform well?

How do the habits of these people compare to having a strong faith and a close relationship with God?

DID YOU KNOW?

The churches mentioned in Revelation chapter 2 and 3 were real churches in the area now known as Turkey.

Challenge

For a week ask your parents to get you up ten minutes earlier. Spend this time talking to God.

The Christian Life

Family Devotions

49 We grow stronger by praying to God.

TALK about it

Think about a close friend that moved far away. Did you stay close to that person? Why or why not?

Think About It

How do you stay close to your friends? When we spend time together and talk often, we become better friends. Sometimes we take our friends for granted, stop talking, and our friendships are no longer as close. The same thing happens with our relationship with God. He doesn't move away from us; He doesn't ever change. But we move away from Him when we don't talk with Him often. Isaiah 40:31 is a beautiful description of what happens when we stay connected to God. Do you want God's power in your life? Through prayer, stay attached to God.

Memorize It

Now it's time to exercise your mind and your body. Recite each sentence as you do various exercises, changing exercises with each sentence.

But those who hope in the LORD will renew their strength. They will soar on wings like eagles; they will run and not grow weary, they will walk and not be faint.
Isaiah 40:31

Pray About It

Make a family prayer list. Add to it daily. Think of friends & relatives as well as your own needs. Pray for these needs. Depend on God for His strength to supply your needs.

Building Kids Faith Series

The Christian Life

50 Christians help those in need.

- Christians help and care for all their neighbors.
- We express our love for others through acts of compassion.
- Christians help those in need.

What do YOU think?

What kinds of people are easy for you to help? What kinds of people do you try to avoid? Make a list of people you know that could really use help. What kind of help do they need?

Has God given you gifts or resources that you could use to help any of them? How can you help?

DID YOU KNOW?

The book of Revelation quotes the Old Testament more than 30 times.

Challenge

Make a list of people you know that you could help this week.

Scripture

50 Christians help those in need.

TALK about it

Who are the neediest people in our community? Why?

Think About It

Our actions show others that we are believers, and they show others how we should live. Caring for others demonstrates that we care for people and that we love God. We are accused of being hypocrites or liars when we say we love God but don't love our neighbors. The letter of James says it well: "What good is it, my brothers, if a man claims to have faith but has no deeds? Can such faith save him? Suppose a brother or sister is without clothes and daily food. If one of you says to him, 'Go, I wish you well; keep warm and well fed,' but does nothing about his physical needs, what good is it? In the same way, faith by itself, if it is not accompanied by actions, is dead" (James 2:14–17). Do your actions say you love God?

Memorize It

Take turns reading the verse and talking about things that are hard to share. Each day read less and say more from memory and think of things your family will share.

All the believers were together and had everything in common. Selling their possessions and goods, they gave to anyone as he had need.
Acts 2:44–45

Pray About It

Work together to plan one or two service projects you could do as a family. Spend the week planning and praying; pick one project for Friday or Saturday

Building Kids FAITH Series

Scripture

51 Living for Jesus makes life better.

- Living for Jesus makes life better.
- Hope and courage is found in living for Jesus.

What do YOU think?

Pretend there's a bully in your school. He may not be bothering you, but he is bothering others. What do you do to help?

How do you find courage in everyday tough situations? What do you do to make sure you are making wise decisions? Who do you turn to for advice?

DID YOU KNOW?

The word *bible* never appears in the Bible.

Challenge

Think carefully—what are some ways your life could be better? How can Jesus help you reach these goals?

Scripture

51 Living for Jesus makes life better.

TALK about it
When you are afraid or confused, who do you call for help?

Think About It

Check out John 10:10. This is what the Christian life can be for us. This is how it was designed for us. Jesus wants our life to be joyful, not boring. Anytime God says "Don't do that," it is to help us not to hurt us. God tells us we should do something, it is to make our life better, not miserable. Following Jesus should be joyful during good times and peaceful during difficult times. The all-powerful God is there when we feel weak. The all-knowing God is our friend when we need wisdom. The all-loving God promises to never leave us when we are lonely. It's the devil who wants to take away anything good in your life, not God. God has adopted us as His children. Our Father in heaven wants to give us the very best. Trust Him, obey Him, and receive the best. How is life better with God?

Memorize It

Tape a copy of the verse above every faucet in the house. Whenever anyone gets a drink or runs water recite the verse out loud. Do it from memory as soon as possible.

I have told you these things, so that you may have peace. In this world you will have trouble. But take heart! I have overcome the world.
John 16:33

Pray About It

Each day have one person share an idea of how living for Jesus makes our lives better. Ask God to show us how to live to please Him.

Scripture

 52

Jesus will come back and take us to heaven.

- Jesus promises us eternal life.
- As Jesus is preparing a place for us, we must prepare our hearts for Him.
- Jesus will come back and take us to heaven.

What do YOU think?

Think about the perfect place to live. Draw a picture of it.

DID YOU KNOW?

The book of Revelation says that there are "thousands upon thousands, and ten thousand times ten thousand" angels in heaven.

How much better will heaven be?

Challenge

Think of people you know who don't know Jesus. Think of ways you can invite them to the party in heaven.

Building Kids FAITH Series

Scripture

52 Jesus will come back and take us to heaven.

TALK about it
What do you think heaven will look like? Why?

Think About It

When we think about what God has already done for us we do not need to fear heaven. Read Revelation 20–21. This chapter has obviously not been read by all the people who do television commercials with images of heaven and hell. The devil is doomed. He finally gets what is coming to him. Hell is not a place you get to hang out with all your friends and do the things you weren't allowed to do. Hell is a place of punishment for every bad thought and bad action ever done. Hell is no fun at all, and there is a complete absence of any goodness.

Heaven on the other hand is filled with every good thing God can think of to bless His children and bring glory to His name. No tears, no fears. God will provide everything we need.

Are you ready for heaven?

Memorize It

Have each person state one thing they would like to see in heaven and then say this verse. Remind everyone that God will make Heaven even better than we imagine it. Learn this great verse!

. . . .

And if I go and prepare a place for you, I will come back and take you to with me that you also may be where I am.
John 14:3

Pray About It

List the things God has made for us that are beautiful and wonderful. Add to the list daily. Read the list and thank God for what He has made.

According to Barna Research Group, most of a child's moral and spiritual foundation is in place by age nine. Don't miss this opportune time to influence the next generation with Bible truths.

Each book in the Building Faith Kids series contains 52 lessons that effectively communicate basic doctrines of the Christian faith to preschool, elementary, or middle school children. The material is flexible and is ideal for use alongside existing curriculum in Sunday school, children's church, midweek programs, or VBS.

• Comprehensive • Versatile • Easy to Use
• Age Appropriate

LEARNING
About God

Basic Christian Concepts
for Preschoolers

52 Versatile Lesson Plans

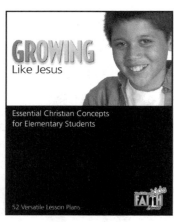

GROWING
Like Jesus

Essential Christian Concepts
for Elementary Students

52 Versatile Lesson Plans

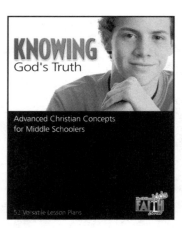

KNOWING
God's Truth

Advanced Christian Concepts
for Middle Schoolers

52 Versatile Lesson Plans

Preschoolers will learn to:
- Treat the Bible with respect.
- Locate the Old and New Testaments.
- Seek forgiveness and accept Jesus as their Savior when ready.
- Help others.
- Forgive others.
- Respect and obey parents.
- Pray.
- Help take care of God's world.
- Bring offerings.
- Invite a friend to church.

Elementary students will learn to:
- Locate a Bible passage by book, chapter, and verse.
- Recite the books of the New Testament.
- Read the Bible and apply it to their lives.
- Pray for others and themselves.
- Recite the Ten Commandments and Lord's Prayer.
- Tell friends about Jesus.
- Trust God to answer prayer.
- Participate in worship.

Middle schoolers will be able to:
- Recite the books of the Old Testament.
- Use a concordance and Bible dictionary.
- Consecrate their lives to God.
- Rely on the Holy Spirit for guidance.
- Tell a friend how to be born again.
- Demonstrate a Christlike attitude.
- Create guidelines to use for making decisions.
- Participate in ministry.

Each Building Faith Kids lesson contains:

- Age-Appropriate Biblical Concept
- Memory Verse
- Session Preparation Guide
- Activity Options
- Prayer Focus
- Action Point
- Bridge to Next Lesson

Subject Areas Taught at Each Level:

- God
- Salvation
- Bible
- The Church
- Self
- The Christian Life
- Jesus

Use Building Faith Kids with your children!

GET CREEPY WITH THE BAILEY SCHOOL KIDS CLUB!

FREE! GLOW-IN-THE-DARK MONSTER NAILS!

MAGAZINE

THE BAILEY SCHOOL KIDS MAGAZINE
The Real Scoop On Gargoyles
A Hunchback of Notre Dame Poster!

OFFICIAL MONSTER PACK $2.95 PLUS SHIPPING AND HANDLING

Gargoyles Don't Drive School Buses
Who is this strange new teacher?

2 BOOKS

Skeletons Don't Play Tubas
Band class can be bone-chilling!

by Debbie Dadey and Marcia Thornton Jones

MEMBERSHIP CARD

The Bailey School Kids Joke Book

JOKE BOOK

◄ DETACH ◄

POSTER

WATCH OUT!
There are more spooky tales going on in Bailey City...

BOOKENDS

☐ YES, please enroll me in The Adventures of the Bailey School Kids Club

(8M3K1A)

Send my introductory 8-piece monster pack for the introductory offer price of $2.95 (plus shipping and handling). Then every month, for as long as I like, I will continue to receive new packs—each with two more Bailey School Kids books, the next Bailey School Kids magazine and a monster-ous activity—for just $7.95 (plus shipping and handling and applicable sales tax). I may cancel at any time.

☐ Boy ☐ Girl   Mo_____ Day_____ Year_____   _____
                              Birthday   Grade

First Name   Last Name
_____

Address   (print in ink)
_____

City   State   Zip
_____

(_____) _____
Telephone Number

_____
Parent's Signature (must be signed)

Offer valid in U.S. zip-coded address only. Limit one per child.

The Adventures of THE BAILEY SCHOOL KIDS

GET CREEPY WITH THE BAILEY SCHOOL KIDS CLUB!

FREE! GLOW-IN-THE-DARK MONSTER NAILS!

Your Official Monster Pack includes:

- *Gargoyles Don't Drive School Buses*
- *Skeletons Don't Play Tubas*
- *The Bailey School Kids Joke Book*

- The Bailey School Kids Magazine
- Bailey School Kids Bookends
- Mysterious Membership Card
- Monster-ous Poster   *Plus...*

- **FIVE GLOW-IN-THE-DARK MONSTER NAILS FREE!**

BUSINESS REPLY MAIL

FIRST-CLASS MAIL   PERMIT NO. 670   CLIFTON, NJ

POSTAGE WILL BE PAID BY ADDRESSEE

BAILEY SCHOOL KIDS CLUB
SCHOLASTIC INC.
P.O. BOX 5014
CLIFTON, NJ 07015-9592

NO POSTAGE
NECESSARY
IF MAILED
IN THE
UNITED STATES

Join today!

This introductory pack will arrive at your home 4-6 weeks after you fill out and mail the attached order card. Don't forget to get your parent's signature.

Great Savings!

For as long as you like you will continue to receive new packs— each with two more Bailey School Kids books, the next Bailey School Kids magazine and a monsterous activity—for just $7.95 (plus shipping and handling). You can cancel at any time.

No risk...

To enjoy this gift-packed, free trial invitation, simply detach, complete with parent's signature, and return the postage-paid, FREE Trial Invitation form on the other side.

Respond today!

Offer expires December 31, 1998

9

Home for Hercules

"There he is," Melody whispered as Dr. Herb came out of the office building.

"We can't follow him," Liza said as the last bit of sunlight faded in the sky. "Eddie isn't here yet."

"Maybe he decided not to come," Howie said. "After all, he didn't believe us."

"But Eddie loves to spy," Liza said. "We should wait for him."

"If we don't follow Dr. Herb now," Melody said, "we'll never know where he lives."

Melody, Liza, and Howie stayed in the shadows as they walked down Green Street past the Bailey City Mall. Dr. Herb whistled as he walked and never once looked behind him. On his shoulder, Dr.

41

Herb carried a huge suitcase that was big enough to hold a ten-year-old kid.

"I don't like this," Liza whispered. They were right across from the Bailey City Cemetery when a dog barked. Another dog barked, then another. Finally, three dogs barked together.

"Maybe that's Cerb, Cerb, and Cerb," Liza whimpered.

Howie put his hand on Liza's shoulder. "I thought you didn't believe in three-headed dogs," he said.

"When it starts to get dark and I'm right beside a cemetery, anything is possible," Liza said with a gulp. "I want to go home."

"We can't leave now," Melody said. "I think Dr. Herb is almost home." She pointed ahead to Dr. Herb. He turned onto Olympus Lane.

"Wow," Howie said. "He really is rich." Olympus Lane only had a few houses on it, and every house was like a palace. Dr. Herb went up the driveway of a huge

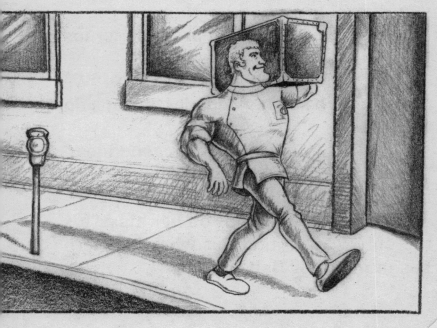

three-story home that had at least ten columns holding up the porch roof.

"Of course he's rich," Melody said. "He is the son of a king."

"King?" Liza asked. "I thought he was the son of a dentist."

Melody rolled her eyes. "Didn't you read my trading cards? Zeus was the king of all the Greek gods and Hercules was Zeus' son."

"Cool," Howie said. "That means royalty cleaned your teeth. Does a queen cut your hair?"

Liza giggled. "Maybe a princess scrubs your toilets."

"Very funny," Melody snapped. "We came here to spy on Hercules, so let's do it."

"I don't think this is such a good idea," Liza said. "Spying is not very nice. It might even be against the law."

Melody put her hands on her hips. "It's the only way to find out what Dr. Herb has in mind for Bailey City."

"And *if* he's really Hercules," Howie added. "Besides, we're not going to hurt anybody."

Liza nodded. "I suppose you're right."

"Be quiet," Melody told her friends. "We have to keep our eyes and ears open for anything unusual."

The three kids were silent for a minute, watching the lights come on in the big house, when suddenly Liza pulled on Melody's sleeve. "Would something moving in the bushes be unusual?" Liza squeaked.

"Sure," Melody said. "Where are the bushes moving?"

Liza looked ready to faint. "Right behind us." Liza gulped. "And whatever it is, it's getting closer!"

10

One Bite

"Oh, my gosh," Liza squealed. "It's Cerberus and it's going to eat us alive!"

Howie's face was pale. "Cerberus could swallow all three of us in one bite."

Melody grabbed a stick from the ground. "It's not going to make me doggie kibble without a fight." Liza and Howie grabbed sticks, too, and held them up like King Arthur's knights with swords.

"Great," Howie said with a trembling voice. "All we have to fight off a dragon-eating monster with are these little toothpicks."

"Let's hope it is a dragon-eating monster and not a kid-eating monster," Liza said as the bushes right beside them shook.

All three kids jumped as a figure leaped out of the bushes at them.

"AHHH!" they screamed.

"Shhh," Eddie said. "Do you want everyone on Olympus Lane to know we're here?"

"Eddie," Liza scolded. "You almost gave me a heart attack. I thought you were a killer dog."

"My grandmother thinks I'm a mad dog," Eddie said with a grin. "But that's only when I'm foaming at the mouth with toothpaste."

Melody punched Eddie in the arm. "What's the big idea of sneaking up on us like that?" she asked.

"I got to Dr. Herb's building just as you were leaving, so I followed you," Eddie explained. "Have you seen anything yet?"

Howie shook his head. "It just looks like an ordinary rich person's house to me."

"Maybe these will help," Eddie said, holding up a big pair of black binoculars. "They're my dad's." Eddie lifted the binoculars to his eyes and concentrated on Dr. Herb's house.

"Wow," Eddie said. "That box Dr. Herb carried home is big enough for . . ."

"Big enough for what?" Liza asked.

"Big enough to put one of his patients in," Eddie said seriously.

"I don't think Hercules ever really hurt anyone, did he?" Melody asked.

"You can't be the strongest man in the world and fight battles without knocking a few heads together," Howie said.

"Shhh," Eddie said. "Dr. Herb is doing something."

"Is he beating up somebody?" Liza asked.

"No," Eddie said. "He's dusting."

"Dusting!" Melody, Liza, and Howie exclaimed together.

"What kind of muscle man dusts?" Melody said.

Eddie continued staring through the binoculars. "A very boring one," Eddie said. "I told you he's just a dumb old dentist."

"What's he dusting?" Melody asked.

"Old stuff," Eddie said. "It looks like an old sword, a globe, and this big gold crown on a stand."

"A prince would have a crown," Howie said.

"It's just a piece of junk," Eddie said. "It must be a zillion years old. Wait! Now he's doing something exciting."

"Is he putting on the crown?" Liza asked.

Eddie frowned and put down his binoculars. "He may be a dentist, but he's not a sissy. He's lifting weights."

"What's wrong with that?" Liza said.

Eddie pulled off his baseball cap and scratched his head. "Maybe Dr. Herb really is Hercules," he said. "I just saw him lift more weights than ten men could lift. And he did it with one hand."

51

"Let me see those binoculars," Melody said, grabbing them away from Eddie. Melody peered through the binoculars at Dr. Herb.

"What's he doing now?" Liza asked.

Melody gulped before answering. "He's coming out the door and heading straight toward us!"

11

Magic Number

"Let's get out of here," Howie said.

"Run!" Eddie yelled. Eddie cut through the bushes and raced into the dark shadows of the cemetery.

"Where are you going?" Melody screamed.

"This is a shortcut," Eddie hollered over his shoulder. "Follow me."

Melody, Howie, and Liza zigzagged through the cemetery after their friend. Melody and Howie kept up with Eddie, but Liza fell behind. Soon, her friends were out of sight.

"Stop!" Liza panted. "Wait for me!" Liza leaned against a tree. She crouched low and held her breath when she heard footsteps pounding the dirt.

"Liza?" Melody hissed through the darkness. "Where did you go?"

Liza let out her breath with a big whoosh. "I'm over here," she whispered.

Melody, Howie, and Eddie appeared in front of Liza. "Why did you stop?" Eddie snapped.

Melody pulled on Eddie's shirt until he plopped down on the ground next to her. "We need to rest," Melody said. "Or Hercules will catch us for sure."

"The only person that's going to catch us is a mad dentist," Eddie told her.

"Why did you run if you didn't believe he's Hercules?" Liza asked.

"Because the last person I want mad at me is a dentist," Eddie said.

"Maybe he didn't see us," Liza said hopefully. But no one answered her because just then they heard something that sent goose bumps racing up their backs. Three different dogs were barking, and they were heading their way.

"Hercules is siccing Cerberus on us,"

Melody said. "We have to get out of here."

"If that really is Cerberus and Hercules, we might as well give up," Liza said. "We can't outrun monsters like that!"

"No," Eddie said. "But we can outwit them!"

Melody, Liza, and Howie stared at their friend. "*You* plan to outwit them?" Melody asked.

Eddie sat up straight. "I'm not stupid," he said. "I happen to have lots of good ideas."

"Yes," Liza admitted. "But most of your ideas are mean or downright danger-ous."

"Not this one," Eddie said. "All we have to do is split up in four directions and make our way to the oak tree on the playground."

"What good will that do?" Liza said.

"I get it," Howie said. "Cerberus may have three heads, but he only has one body. Splitting up will confuse him."

Melody nodded. "I hope it works."

"We're about to find out," Howie said, "because Cerberus is almost here. Let's go!"

The four friends raced away in different directions. They hadn't gone far when they heard the barks change into yelps and whimpers. When the kids met up under the oak tree they were out of breath, but they were all right.

"Eddie," Liza said, "I owe you an apology. Your plan was brilliant!"

Eddie smiled and gave a little bow.

"Don't start bragging," Melody said, "unless you have another plan for getting rid of Hercules for good."

"Eddie doesn't have to think of a plan," Howie said slowly, "because I just thought of something. Twelve seems to be a magic number for Dr. Herb and Hercules," Howie explained. "We know Melody was

Dr. Herb's tenth patient. What happens when he gets to patient number twelve?"

Eddie shrugged. "I guess we'll never know," he said.

"Yes, we will," Howie said with a grin. "Because I plan on being patient eleven."

"Well, if you're patient eleven, who will be twelve?" Eddie asked.

Melody, Liza, and Howie didn't say a word. Instead, they stared at Eddie.

Eddie's hands covered his mouth. "You can't be serious," he said through his fingers.

"We're serious," Melody said slowly. "Deadly serious!"

12

Patient Number Twelve

"I can't believe you're making me do this," Eddie grumbled. "My grandmother took my temperature when I told her I was making an appointment with a dentist. She thought I was sick with a fever."

Eddie and his friends Melody, Howie, and Liza were riding the elevator up to the twelfth floor. Howie had already made an appointment for right after school. Eddie was going to make his appointment when they got there. The elevator doors slid open and the four friends quietly walked into office 1212. Howie, Liza, and Melody stood with Eddie while he made an appointment. Then Howie told the receptionist he was ready.

"What if he starts drilling holes in my teeth?" Eddie asked.

Liza giggled. "A few more holes in your head shouldn't hurt anything!"

"This is nothing to laugh about," Eddie told her. "I could be hurt in there!"

Liza's eyes got big, then she started giggling.

"Now what's so funny?" Melody asked.

"Who would ever have thought," Liza gasped, "that Eddie's afraid of the dentist!"

"I am not," Eddie snapped.

"Then stop worrying," Liza told him. "Dr. Herb is as gentle as a kitten when he's cleaning teeth."

Howie snapped his fingers. "I just thought of another plan, and if it works Eddie won't have to worry about seeing the dentist. At least, not today."

"What are you going to do?" Melody asked.

Howie didn't answer her because the door leading to the examining rooms swung open and Dr. Herb grinned down at the four friends. "I am ready for you now," Dr. Herb said. "Please, follow me."

Howie slowly followed Dr. Herb. He squeezed past the three-headed dog statue and slid into the dentist's chair. Before Dr. Herb could begin cleaning his teeth, Howie started talking. "You really have big muscles," he told Dr. Herb.

"I work out with weights," Dr. Herb said. Then he pinched Howie's skinny arm. "I could teach you how to work your muscles if you'd like."

Howie sighed. "I could never be as strong as you. I bet you could lift an entire car."

Dr. Herb flexed one of his muscles. "I do like a challenge," he admitted.

"Of course," Howie said quietly, "you couldn't straighten the leaning tower of Pisa in Italy. And it would be too hard for you to rebuild that crumbling coliseum in Rome."

Howie noticed that Dr. Herb was frowning.

"There's a great big hole called the Grand Canyon," Howie said. "But filling that hole is just like fixing the coliseum and the tower. They're all jobs that even the strongest man in the world couldn't do. It would be too big of a challenge."

Dr. Herb scratched his chin as if he were thinking very hard. Then Dr. Herb leaned over Howie and went to work without saying a word.

13

Follow Your Dreams

The next morning Howie, Melody, and Liza rang Eddie's doorbell. They had to wait a long time before the door finally opened.

"Hurry up," Howie said. "You'll be late for your dentist appointment."

Eddie shook his head. "I'm not going," he said. "There's no way I'm letting that muscle man mess with my molars."

"You're his twelfth patient," Melody said.

"That's exactly why I'm not going," Eddie said.

"You have to go," Liza told him. "It wouldn't be polite to miss your appointment."

With his three friends pushing him the entire way, Eddie slowly made his way to

Dr. Herb's office. Silently, he pressed the button for the twelfth floor. By the time he reached office 1212, Eddie's face was as white as the teeth in his mouth.

As soon as the four kids entered the office, they knew something was wrong.

"The pictures are missing," Melody whispered. She was right. Not a single picture of a dog was left on the wall.

The receptionist called Eddie, but Eddie stopped before disappearing down the long hallway.

"You're not going to let me go by myself, are you?" Eddie asked.

But his friends didn't have a chance to answer because just then, a loud voice echoed into the waiting room. "Of course your friends can come with you," said the friendly voice.

"Dr. Zeus!" Liza screamed. "You're back."

Dr. Zeus stepped into the waiting room and grinned at the four friends. "I had to come back," he said. "I missed my patients too much!"

Eddie reached out and shook Dr. Zeus's hand so hard the white-haired man laughed. "I never thought I'd see the day when kids like you would be happy to see a dentist!"

"It's not just any dentist," Melody said. "We're happy to see *you!*"

"But what happened to Dr. Herb?" Howie asked. "He was supposed to check Eddie's teeth."

Dr. Zeus scratched his chin and shrugged. "I believe he found another job," he said, "in Italy."

"*Italy?*" Howie gasped. But Dr. Zeus didn't hear because he had already walked down the hall.

"My plan worked," Howie told Liza and Melody. "Dr. Herb has left Bailey City."

"But what if he comes back?" Liza asked.

"I don't think we'll see Dr. Herb for a long, long time," Howie said. "He'll be gone at least a couple of centuries."

"How do you know that?" Eddie asked.

Howie smiled. "Remember those cards Melody had?"

Liza and Eddie nodded. Melody pulled a stack of cards from her pocket.

"What do cards have to do with a dentist hightailing it out of his office?" Eddie asked.

"The cards told about Hercules' liking superhuman challenges," Howie said. "So I gave Hercules some challenges he couldn't resist."

"Thank goodness," Melody said. "Bailey City is safe now."

Eddie grabbed Melody's cards and held up the one of a creature with wild hair that looked like snakes. "We're okay," Eddie joked, "until Melody finds someone with crazy hair like this!"

Debbie Dadey and Marcia Thornton Jones have fun writing stories together. When they both worked at an elementary school in Lexington, Kentucky, Debbie was the school librarian and Marcia was a teacher. During their lunch break in the school cafeteria, they came up with the idea of the Bailey School kids.

Recently Debbie and her family moved to Aurora, Illinois. Marcia and her husband still live in Kentucky where she continues to teach. How do these authors still write together? They talk on the phone and use computers and fax machines!

Creepy, weird, wacky and funny things happen to the Bailey School Kids!™ Collect and read them all!

The Adventures of
THE BAILEY SCHOOL KIDS®